Precious
as
Silver

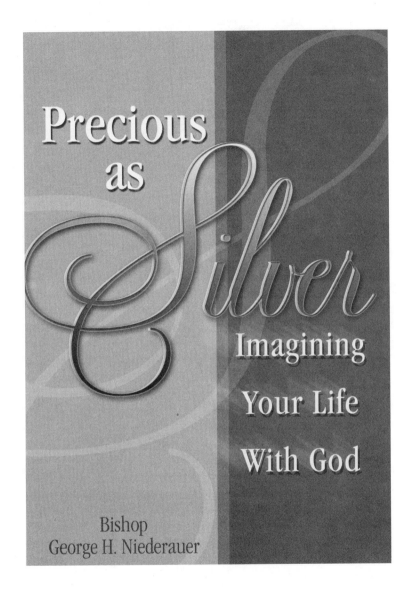

Precious as Silver

Imagining Your Life With God

Bishop
George H. Niederauer

ave maria press AmP Notre Dame, Indiana

© 2004 by Ave Maria Press,™ Inc.

www.avemariapress.com

International Standard Book Number: 0-87793-998-5

Cover and text design by Katherine Robinson Coleman

Printed and bound in the United States of America

Library of Congress Cataloging-in-Publication Data

Niederauer, George (George H.)
  Precious as silver : imagining your life with God / George Niederauer.
       p. cm.
Includes bibliographical references.
  ISBN 0-87793-998-5 (pbk.)
  1. Christian life—Catholic authors. 2. Spiritual life—Christianity. I. Title.
  BX2350.3.N54 2003
  248.4'82—dc22
                                                                2003021521

Contents

Introduction

*H*ere's an image to begin with: Many years ago I glanced at a picture on the back of a paperback. I don't remember the book at all, but the image has stayed with me. It was a silhouette of an old man standing under a tree, leaning on a cane. The caption read: "Inside every old man is a young man, wondering what happened."

That's my own experience as I grow older. I still feel young and new in many ways. The past still remains fresh, so much in the present fascinates me, while the future intrigues me. Much of me is slower and graying, but not my heart.

My life as a disciple of Jesus Christ is that way too. So are the lives of many Christians. That's because the direction of faith is forward in time, not backward, and the wonder of the lively crib and the empty tomb can astonish us all our lives long, if we let it.

But along with wonder and belief come questions. Having questions is not a new experience for disciples of Jesus Christ. We have that in common with Peter, Philip, and Andrew, as well as with disciples in every generation of the church that followed them.

Our most important questions concern our lives in Christ. They spring from our efforts to live in the world as disciples, guided by the Spirit of Jesus. This book is about some of those questions.

We begin with the question, How do we "see" God? Is he loving, just, and challenging, or does he seem to rule us by guilt, shame, judgment, and endless exhausting demands? How does God see us? Are we precious to him in spite of our imperfections, in spite of being unfinished? Or are we disappointing to our Creator, valuable only as yes persons, doing all the work he can get out of us?

How does God treat us, now and in eternity? If God is as loving as some believers claim, then what explains human suffering? Is God in control of our lives, or are we? Is there a plan? And what about eternal life?

What should a disciple of Jesus be like? How does the Lord expect his followers to act? How do we choose kingdom values rightly, and how do we go wrong?

If we are taking the Christian life seriously, how do we listen and talk to God without trying to control him or without giving up and running away? That is, how do we pray? How do we serve God in the church without becoming proud, judgmental, or selfish loners? How do we minister to each other, side by side, in servant fashion?

These are some of our most basic questions about God and the kingdom. When Jesus addressed such questions, he often used images: weeds, wheat, pearls, yeast, kings, banquets, a lost sheep, and the like. Why did Jesus use images? Why not just develop a question-and-answer catechism?

Incarnation is why. When God set out to save us, he didn't just send us a book—he came himself. Jesus Christ is the Word of God made flesh like us. His first followers could see and hear and touch him, before and after he died and rose. Even now our most powerful contact with

Christ is not through words on a page, but in the bread and wine of Eucharist—solid, visible, touchable things. We are flesh and blood, and God knows that flesh-and-blood experiences speak to us more immediately than theories and concepts.

As a good teacher, Jesus knew the best way to answer questions: not with abstract ideas but with an appeal to human experience. Good teachers are always appealing to our experience. Over forty years ago a professor of mine was asked whether he favored liberals or conservatives in government. He replied, "That's like asking whether I want an accelerator or brakes on my car." He could have spent an hour talking about political theory, but with that concrete image he laid out the basics of his answer in a few seconds. He could later build everything else on that flash of insight. That's how good teaching often works.

Of course scholars and theologians have much to teach us about the subtle and profound implications of Jesus and his gospel. Still, in our daily pilgrimage, as we disciples face questions about our faith, the best thing we can do is to visit again the teachings of Jesus in the gospel, filled with images of daily life.

However, we are not confined to gospel images. The good news of the kingdom is a living, developing reality. Each generation of disciples finds new ways to interpret and apply the teachings of Christ to its own experience. Today Christ still speaks powerfully through scriptural images, but he can also teach us through images drawn from our daily lives: construction sites, silverware, fictional characters, and park benches, among others. I will use such images to address the questions we have as disciples of the Lord.

First, though, let's consider what an image actually is. In our time the very word "image" has an image problem! Until recently "image" was an honorable word.

Catechisms taught that we were made "in the image and likeness of God." Presently, however, "image" can suggest a manipulative trick, a fooling around with external appearances, something superficial used to create a false impression of a politician, a sports car, or a lunchtime snack. In an unguarded moment during a political campaign, a spin doctor once said, "People don't care about the issues. All that matters is the image."

That's a dreadful political philosophy. However, in a profoundly human sense, the image *is* what matters. We think, imagine, and remember in images. That's why Jesus taught us in parables. When we disciples ask our questions, we use images to look for answers.

I am using the word "image" here in almost all its shades of meaning. Most obviously, we fashion images of what we love or respect or wonder at, in stone, in paint, in photograph albums. We represent God and the saints in our churches, just as we carry snapshots of our families in our wallets. Ordinarily we do not confuse any of those images with the real thing.

Indeed, "image" suggests even more than that. We glimpse an image of ourselves as we pass a mirror. We hear someone speak, or we read a book, and a description brings some remote reality to life for us. A song, a play, or a film can have the same effect. Perhaps we meet someone who concretizes a human experience for us: "She was the very picture of grief." In each of these instances, the image in some way portrays or "stands in for" the idea, the person, the relationship, or the situation.

Such "pictures in the mind" are what I want to offer here, and they come from the scriptures, from other disciples, from literature, and from daily life. I will use such images to address our deepest questions as disciples: What is God like? What do we seem like to God? How does God deal with us? What kind of disciples does Jesus want us to be? More particularly, how does Jesus call us to pray and to serve in his kingdom? Images have helped me to wrestle with and wonder at the mystery of grace without trying to control it or pin it down. I hope they can help other disciples of the Lord in similar ways. In the course of each chapter, I have suggested scripture passages for praying and reflecting further on the question or image.

In no way do I intend to offer a comprehensive treatment of these important questions. These are ancient issues for Christians, and each has already been dealt with at greater length and in greater depth by theologians and spiritual writers, and will be again. However, the images offered here have been helpful to me and to others in prayer and reflection, and sometimes one of them has provided a way toward peace and understanding. May they do that for the reader as well.

chapter one

What Is God Like?

*W*hat is our image of God? What is God actually like for us? There may be as many different answers to those questions as there are disciples; indeed, probably more, because within each disciple there may be several different images of God, competing, conflicting, and even combining with one another. For instance, if a teacher says to a classroom of thirty children, "God is like your father," thirty different statements have been heard, some of them possibly quite uncomplimentary to a creating, redeeming, and sanctifying God.

That's always been one of God's problems with his people. Yahweh complained through the Old Testament prophet Ezekiel that his name was "profaned among the nations." God grew angry when he saw his people misinterpreting him as being far away from them, unconcerned with their problems and their sins, unloving, uncaring, uninvolved with them. Again and again God revealed that he loved his people passionately and called them to love him in return. Finally, in Jesus, his Son, God most fully expressed his love for his daughters and sons.

"Gawd"

Still, after two millennia of Christianity, we find it difficult to imagine God cherishing us. We have a persistent problem with false images of God. Perhaps the single most destructive false image of the divine is the one I will call "Gawd." Too many Christians walk around each day with an almost demonic image of God in their minds and hearts. It is often a schizoid vision: I look out of one eye and see Jesus who loves me, meek and gentle Jesus who died and rose for me, who forgives my sins and gives himself to me in Eucharist. I look out of the other eye and see "Gawd": a harsh judge, seeing through me to my trashy, pointless core; an unforgiving lord, keeping dreadful score, uninvolved with my suffering, perhaps punishing me with it. "Gawd" is the eternal highway patrolman in the sky, hidden behind the billboards of life, waiting to catch me and condemn me.

Does that sound overwrought? If only it were. Language is coded with our assumptions, and it provides us with a quick test for the presence of this divided image of God. When was the last time you said, or heard someone say, "Why is God doing this to me? Why is God letting this happen?" Probably not so long ago. Now let's change the question slightly. When was the last time you said, or heard someone else say: "Why is Jesus doing this to me? Why is Jesus letting this happen?" Perhaps you've never said or heard that. Why? Because Jesus is the good one; it's God we have to watch out for. That's one version of the image of "Gawd."

Often we draw our image of God out of our own sinful pessimism and not from revelation, from his own self-disclosure. Voltaire remarked that ever since God made us in his own image we have been trying to return the compliment. He was uncomfortably right about many of us. How blithely we can assume that we know precisely the judgment of God.

Consider this: Unless we have had far too much to drink, we would never go to a party, approach someone famous whom we had never seen before, and say, "Oh, I've heard all about you. I know exactly what you're like. You don't need to say a word. I'll bet I know what you think about everything!" On the contrary, we know that each human being is too complicated and mysterious to be fully known and understood by another. Do we believe that God is not?

In a rage to pin God down and get him straight, many disciples have come up with a "good cop/bad cop" image of God. Jesus is the good one. He's on our side, staying the Father's hand, so we won't be punished and damned—most of the time. It's a dreadful arrangement, but at least it's neat and clear. Is it true? Fortunately not, according to God.

At the Last Supper, Jesus spoke at length about his Father. The disciple Philip said, "Master, show us the Father, and that will be enough for us." Jesus seemed disappointed, perhaps even a bit hurt: "Have I been with you for so long a time and you still do not know me, Philip? Whoever has seen me has seen the Father. How can you say, 'Show us the Father'? Do you not believe that I am in the Father and the Father is in me?" (John 14:8–10).

That's the good news about what God is really like, the revealing light that pierces the gloom of our false images. We have it straight from God: there is no "Gawd." Instead, there is a loving, creating Father, a redeeming Son, fully human like us and fully divine, and the Spirit of their love and life. That's all the God Christians get or need. If we want to know what God the Father is like, we need to look at his Son and listen to him—there's a family resemblance. What's more, we share in that resemblance through our baptisms and our lives as disciples.

Does the true image of God in Christ Jesus explain away all our questions about his will and our sufferings, and countless other matters? Certainly not. Nevertheless, this true image is the context within which we face those realities and questions. Think of it this way: Once we are sure of a friend's goodness and honesty and love for us, does that eliminate every possible misunderstanding or disagreement between us? No, but it makes them all bearable and approachable, and worth bearing and approaching. We don't have all the answers we will ever want just because we know that God feels and thinks and acts about things and people exactly as Jesus does in the gospels. However, we have something better: the beginning of such a beautiful and eternal friendship that we won't need to fear any question or answer again.

Pause & Pray

Isaiah 43:1–2 Fear not, for I have redeemed you; I have called you by name: you are mine.

Isaiah 49:15 Can a mother forget her infant, be without tenderness for the child of her womb? Even should she forget, I will never forget you.

Jeremiah 29:11 For I know well the plans I have in mind for you, says the Lord, plans for your welfare, not for woe! plans to give you a future full of hope.

Luke 12:6–7 Even the hairs of your head have been counted! Do not be afraid.

Someone may object, "Very well, there is no 'Gawd.' Still, what about the Ten Commandments? Don't they reveal a God who is always saying 'Thou shalt' or 'Thou shalt not'? That doesn't sound much like the loving, creating divine friend you are describing."

It's a mistake to assume that only religion imposes commandments. There are many kinds of commandments all around us in the world, but we have to watch for them to notice them. Television ads are full of commandments: Thou shalt be successful in life; Thou shalt have incredibly white teeth; Thou shalt be popular at all costs; Thou shalt drive the most expensive sports car thou can't afford. There's a special TV commandment for parents and grandparents who are about my age: Thou shalt look young forever if thou wants to go on mattering to anybody. Those are very tough commandments to keep. Young people in school hear equally difficult commandments: Thou shalt be a terrific athlete to be important; Thou shalt not be or look different in any way, if thou knowest what is good for thee.

Sometimes those commandments sound like the most important ones, and if we are not careful we can let them run our lives. But which commandment does God think is the most important? God's Son, Jesus Christ, tells us which is the greatest commandment: "You shall love the Lord, your God, with all your heart, with all your soul, and with all your mind." And Jesus teaches that the second great commandment is like the first: "You shall love your neighbor as yourself" (Matthew 22:37, 39).

Notice that Jesus did not say, "You shall love the Lord, your God, with your perfect complexion, with all your bank accounts, with all your muscles, with your popularity, with all your funny remarks." No, God loves us in our hearts, in our souls, inside the very core of each of us, where no one else sees. God loves us there and wants us to love him back from that core inside us. If God asks us not to lie or steal or kill or be unfaithful, he does so because he knows what kills love and what gives it life.

Pause & Pray

Matthew 22:34–40 Jesus teaches the two greatest commandments.

Jesus Christ Is the Loving Intruder

We Christians believe that a loving Father calls us to listen to his beloved Son and to come to know all the persons of the Trinity in Jesus Christ. This mystery of Incarnation— God's taking flesh in the Crucified One—is a true stumbling block, and not just for Jews and Greeks of the first century of Christianity (1 Corinthians 1:23). Dostoyevsky's Grand Inquisitor restated part of the Pharisees' objection to Jesus Christ for the nineteenth century, and George Bernard Shaw railed against the irrationality of "Crosstianity" in the twentieth. When a crowd tried to stone Jesus, they told him it was because, "You, a man, are making yourself God" (John 10:33).

But that is not the worst of it; any mad person can claim to be God. The truly disturbing action is not a man making himself God; it is God making himself human. The implications of this loving intrusion are never-ending, as is the temptation to avoid them.

If God has become human with us and for us in order to transform our meaning and our fate, then that is the supreme fact of each life. It is the light in which we are to see, evaluate, and respond to everything and everyone. Jesus becomes our point of reference, true north on our compass. "Through him, with him, and in him" becomes a way of life for the disciple. Jesus Christ is not God sidling up to us and occasionally whispering of love. He is God breaking into our lives to stay.

That state of affairs is not as attractive as it might sound. Isn't it often more tempting to imagine a God who creates us, gives us a rule book, and sends us out to make our way in the world? We would be on our own for a lifetime, making friends, enemies, money, love, mistakes, and the like, and then there would be a great summing up, followed by rewards and punishments. "Gawd" fits into that scenario very well. Jesus, his Father, and their Spirit do not.

That's the crucial point. *The* God, the one who loves us passionately, has drawn us into divine life and filled us with his presence, so that we may love and serve our Creator with mind, heart, and soul, centered in union with Jesus the Son and with one another. This kind of closeness can crowd us, unless we recognize it for what it is—not intrusion or invasion but salvation and fulfillment such as we could never know on our own.

Still, we do have to lose our lives to find them (Mark 8:35). We do have to let go of the self-made persons we could have become on our own. Instead of these self-made persons, we find the selves we never could have become by ourselves, when we let Jesus, and his Father, and their Spirit make us into the persons they have called us to become.

Jesus is our mediator, our bridge to the life of God. He is human like us, so he knows from experience what our limitations and yearnings feel like. He is God's Son, sharing the Father's life with us, sending the Spirit of his love to give us light and strength for our lives. We face challenges, failures, and uncertainties daily, and we are tempted to tell God, "I can't do it!" Jesus responds, "Of course you can't—by yourself. But in me, with me, you can." Faith in Christ's saving love for us gives us the power to hope in him, and to return his love.

Jesus Christ is the image of the God who is; he is also the model of the persons we seek to become. But what is Jesus like? That seems to be a much easier question than "What is God like?" but it too has its complications. Fortunately, we have the gospels and letters of the New Testament, devoted to portraying Jesus and his meaning for us, and we have the church's teachings, and generations of believers and witnesses who have gone before us.

Even so, the complications remain. Because the gospel images are so familiar, we need to open ourselves again and again to their freshness and immediacy. Since those images are filtered through the faith experience of other persons, we need to make their meaning our own. Wonderful people can lead us to Jesus and the power of their experience of him, but eventually we have to make our own acts of faith, hope, and love for ourselves.

Recall the encounter in John's gospel between Jesus and the Samaritan woman at the well. She told all the people in her town of his knowledge and love of her, and of her faith in him. Her strong influence on them started them on the path toward faith in Christ.

So they begged Jesus to stay in the town a while. Notice, though, what her neighbors told the woman after two days: "We no longer believe because of your word; for we have heard for ourselves, and we know that this is truly the savior of the world" (John 4:42). Like his disciples, all of us need to listen to Jesus and hear him for ourselves, and to come to know that he really is our Savior, and the Savior of the world.

When we watch and listen to Jesus, the image of the Father, what do we see and hear? We begin in the gospels. There we meet Jesus, the teacher who challenges us to believe in his Father, in himself, and in the kingdom he proclaims. He is the prophet who instills hope in himself and in his new way, new values, new life. Jesus is also the shepherd who compels our love for God and for one another by his life as well as his teaching.

Jesus is a compassionate man who is nonetheless direct, honest, and challenging, with his friends as well as with those who make themselves his enemies. The people around Jesus know where they stand with this man, or they can quickly find out. His origins and his destiny may be a mystery, but the man himself is no puzzle. Jesus is clear about who he is and who he is not, about what he favors and what he is against.

Jesus Is the Lover Who Can Say No

God's love for us is radical and uncompromising, and Jesus expresses such love dramatically in the gospels. This image of Jesus as the divine lover clashes with some of our own human images of love. Our romantic songs, movies, and novels show us lovers who can deny each other nothing. Romantically speaking, to say no to someone I love is seen somehow as a failure to love enough.

Because Jesus rejected no one, we might imagine that he never said no. Often we tell ourselves that a real Christian, following the example of Jesus, never disappoints others, always meets their expectations, and regards saying no as a failure. If we suffer from an image of God as simply our taskmaster, we naturally see Jesus as the perfect worker to whom the Father compares us unfavorably.

Certainly, Jesus was the one for others par excellence, but he was also fully human; he knew how to say no as well as yes, and he did so, yet never sinfully. In fact, each yes and no of Jesus pleased the Father. As we take a closer look at the Jesus who said no, we may discover that our efforts to flog ourselves onward to ever more yeses may not really be so Christlike. We may find out that Jesus, our bridge to the Father's life and love, teaches us a saving lesson about yes, no, and God's will.

Saint Paul wrote to the Corinthians: "Jesus Christ . . . was not 'yes' and 'no,' but 'yes' has been in him" (2 Corinthians 1:19). If Jesus was always yes, what does that mean for his disciples? As Christians, must we be prepared to answer yes to every demand or request, in every situation, no matter what the circumstances? Should we feel selfish or lazy with each no that we say? Often we feel we can't squeeze one more commitment or activity into our lives. Are the alternatives either to let Jesus down or to self-destruct on yeses? In the four gospels is there an image of the Jesus who said no?

Indeed there is. Jesus did not teach or live the extremes described above. True, as Saint Paul said, Jesus was always yes—to his Father's loving will. In turn, we disciples are called always to be yes to Jesus and our Father. We need to listen carefully to this call, and to interpret it correctly. Being and saying yes to the Lord can involve saying no to ourselves and others, even to apparently legitimate demands for a yes.

Many of us find it difficult to get this matter right in our daily living. We may confuse being a good Christian with being a yes person and pleasing everybody all the time. If everyone does not always go away from us perfectly satisfied, we feel sure we have failed. Our need to please others is not God's fault, but sometimes we are tempted to blame him for it. As an antidote to this confusion, it is helpful to read through the four gospels looking for the times when Jesus said no.

Jesus did say no, and not only to Satan three times in the desert. Jesus said no or its equivalent whenever a yes did not fit in with his yes to his Father. The instances are many. Jesus said no to ordinary human requests: Let me bury my father before I follow you—*No* (Matthew 8). Tell my sister to help me with the housework—*No* (Luke 10). Tell my brother to be fair with me about our inheritance—*No* (Luke 12). Stay in our Capernaum a little longer—*No* (Luke 4). Let me follow you (the cured Gerasene demoniac)—*No* (Mark 5).

Close friends, with apparently the strongest claim on Jesus, asked favors: give my sons a special, privileged place next to you—*No* (Matthew 20). Stop talking about your death like that—*No* (Mark 8). Tell us when the last things will occur—*No* (Acts 1). Call down fire from heaven to destroy those towns that rejected you—*No* (Luke 9).

The crowds also made demands of Jesus: Work a sign for us right here and now—*No* (Matthew 12). Do here in your own town the things we have heard you did in Capernaum—*No* (Luke 4). Give us again today the bread you gave us yesterday—*No* (John 6).

Finally, Jesus responded to many commonsense, law-and-order requests from respectable citizens: Send the crowds away, they're getting hungry—*No* (Luke 9). Keep this crowd quiet—*No* (Luke 19). Make your followers practice fasting as those of John the Baptizer do—*No* (Mark 2). Surely you have some answer to these accusations against you—*No* (Mark 15).

Jesus said no whenever he had to in order to continue his lifelong yes to his Father's loving will. That is the model for us disciples. We need to say daily the right yeses and noes in order to live out our lifelong yes to Jesus and our Father in the Spirit.

It's hard to be sure of which answers are right, and it's often harder to give them. Probably the noes are hardest of all. For example, a disciple of Jesus is called to meet the Lord in prayer, to say yes to his invitation to come aside with him. Therefore the disciple is called to say no to anyone or anything that gets in the way of closeness to the Lord in prayer.

Perhaps that sounds harsh and unrealistic. We are busy, and often we cannot find time for prayer. Jesus was busy too, though, and he found time for prayer. If he did not find the time, he carved it out of the day or night. He calls us to do that too.

How? If our lives flow from appointment books and lists of things to do, then our attitude can be "If you can't beat 'em, join 'em." Why not write the name "Jesus Christ" right in there, alongside the bank and the post office? If doing that sounds or feels strange, perhaps the strange feeling tells us how real Jesus' invitation to pray seems for us, especially when compared to the need to go to the bank or the post office.

The issue here is priorities. There is an assumption behind priorities: there may not be time and energy for everything we have to do. If I have three hours' worth of tasks to do, and five hours within which to do them, I probably don't have to set any priorities, because it doesn't matter which of the tasks I do first. However, if I have five hours' worth of work to do in three hours' time, I had better set priorities.

What if we apply this sense of our priorities to our daily meeting with Jesus? We begin by consciously giving prayer a priority, and then we follow through on it, in the same way we make sure we run our errands or call our friends. Thrusting prayer into the midst of the business of life in this fashion may seem to rob it of its mystery and gentleness and spontaneity. But once we have said enough noes and have disciplined the business of life sufficiently so that we are actually praying daily, there will be time and freedom to respond to prayer's more particular graces.

We Christians have other noes to say. We are called to say no to habits, activities, or involvements that weaken our service to Jesus and to our brothers and sisters in him. We need to say no to laziness and ruts, as well as to spreading ourselves too thin; to say no to relationships that are so demanding that our yeses to the Lord and to those he brings close to us are compromised; to say no to whatever gets in the way of our physical and emotional health— any addiction, whether to alcohol, drugs, food, leisure, or work.

We also need to say no to pride in its many forms: Say no to being a know-it-all, and no to people who want us to tell them what they want to hear. Say no to ourselves, when we want to tell people whatever we feel like saying whether or not it is what they need to hear.

It is important, of course, to say our no for the right reasons. In reaction to the burnout that can result from trying to say yes to everyone every time, a new fad has developed. Often now we are encouraged to say no, but not for Christian motives. Rather, we are urged to take care only of ourselves, first, last, and always, to be preoccupied constantly with the care and feeding of self. Sometimes burnout isn't the problem—but ignition is.

In contrast, Christ calls us to let go and lose ourselves, to deny ourselves and take up our crosses daily as we follow him. We recognize a tension in trying to balance self-denial and a proper stewardship of self, but it is a healthy tension, because it helps us to be honest about, and committed to, both values simultaneously. Christians do not say no to make their lives neat, orderly, and comfortable or to be in control all the time. Rather, we say no to open up in loving vulnerability to the Lord's control and direction.

This list of Christian noes can sound a bit bleak. Still, the right kind of no can be a very loving word, especially as Jesus uses it, and as he calls us to use it as disciples in the service of the kingdom. Christ can fill the word no with love, and he can teach us to do that too, if we let him.

When I listed earlier the times Jesus said no or its equivalent in the gospels, it may have seemed that I didn't leave any out, but I did hold one back until now. As sinful, sometimes fearful disciples, we can find this particular no of Jesus quite consoling to hear. In fact, it may be most consoling when we feel Jesus is saying no to us personally, no matter what we ask. Very early in his public ministry Jesus heard one of his future disciples cry out to him in fear, "Depart from me, Lord, for I am a sinful man" (Luke 5:8). He actually said, "Jesus, get away from me." With Peter's whole future life hanging in the balance, Jesus very firmly, tenderly, lovingly answered no.

Pause & Pray

Luke 12:13 Imagine yourself in the crowd, calling out to Jesus to side with you against someone who has wronged you. How does Jesus respond? Does he perhaps urge reconciliation? How do you respond?

Matthew 19:21 Jesus calls the rich young man to follow him, and the man says no. The cured Gerasene wants to follow the Lord, but he's told to stay where he lives and to give witness there (Mark 5:18–19). What do these scenes say to you about vocation?

Acts 1:6–8 The exact time is not for you to know. You are to be my witnesses . . . even to the ends of the earth. Jesus says no to our knowledge about the end of the world and yes to our being disciples. How do we respond?

Is There a Compromise Jesus?

Jesus Christ is gentle, "meek and humble of heart" (Matthew 11:29), but he can also seem so demanding and uncompromising that we are intimidated. The Gerasenes felt that way about this man who dealt so radically with their possessed neighbor and with their herd of pigs (Luke 8:26–39). Perhaps they would have felt better disposed toward the healer if he had stopped at the cure and not permitted their squealing investments to be driven over the cliff. The Gerasenes were some of the first people to choose between Jesus, on the one hand, and peace and prosperity, on the other. They made the popular choice: they asked him to leave town.

Compromises of all sorts tempt us: moral, spiritual, personal, political, economic, and social. All the time, however, Jesus is uncompromising, and we need him to be uncompromising. If that is hard to understand, imagine for a moment a "compromise Jesus." Picture him with the woman caught in adultery (John 8:3–7), as she cowers before him and the crowd. Then imagine Jesus saying something like this: "If some of you haven't sinned too very much, at least not lately, perhaps you could throw a few of the smaller rocks."

Imagine Jesus calling the rich young man (Matthew 19:21) to go, sell everything, put it into a trust fund, and then follow him for a while to see whether it felt agreeable enough to stay with him. Or imagine the Messiah responding to the Pharisees' rebuke for curing people on the Sabbath (Matthew 12:10–12) by promising to cut down on it gradually, or to limit it to extreme cases only, or to try to schedule healing for sunset, or even later. Those are the responses of a forgettable prophet, one who will die in bed and not on a cross. He's not the Jesus we need, the radical Jesus who challenges us to our roots.

The compromise Jesus is related to another false image of God more prevalent in recent years: the divine pushover in the sky, the "Good Old God," a kind of cosmic sweetheart who could never be angry with anyone, let alone condemn what they do. Even the most wrong-headed, wrong-hearted, and destructive attempts at human living and relating will be fine with Someone Up

27

There Who Likes Everything About Us. "Good Old God" thinks everyone should get an E for effort, or maybe even an A for attempt.

What's wrong with that image of God? Jesus is wrong with it. We have only to look at his treatment of the woman accused of adultery. Jesus does not condemn her, but neither does he say something fuzzily "modern" to her: "I understand, dear. Yours was probably an arranged marriage. No doubt your husband is much older than you, and he travels a great deal. You were lonely, and Jerusalem is a big city. Besides, we know that social mores are changing rapidly all across the empire."

Instead, noting that no one else has condemned her after his challenge to them, Jesus says, "Neither do I condemn you. Go, (and) from now on do not sin anymore" (John 8:11). For Jesus, sin is sin, it calls for repentance and conversion, and there is always compassion, forgiveness, and grace from God. As Christians, we reject the motto "Anything Goes," and say instead, "Everything is grace" (to summarize Ephesians 2:4–10).

Pause & Pray

Luke 7:36–50 Her many sins had been forgiven, hence she was shown great love.

Luke 19:1–10 The forgiven and converted Zacchaeus must pay a price for his earlier greed and injustice. Notice that Jesus does not say to him, "Oh, that's alright, Zacchaeus. Keep your money."

God reveals in Jesus Christ that he loves us radically and unconditionally, that his every yes or no to us is an expression of that love. However, we should not skate past a deeper question about our relationship with the Father and the Son. True enough, Jesus invites us to be as intimately united with his life as branches are with a vine (John 15:1–8). However, is Jesus a vine of which I am content to be nothing but a branch?

The question is not as presumptuous as it sounds. It's a vital question for faith and conversion. Granted, Jesus says he wants to give himself unreservedly to me. Do I want to give myself unconditionally to him? It may sound blasphemous to ask, "Is Jesus enough for me?" But people are dealing with that question all the time. The rich young man was not the last person to turn away sadly because, as good as Jesus looked, the price of self-sacrifice was too high (Mark 10:22).

Disciples will commit themselves unconditionally to Christ when they become convinced of God's unconditional love for them. Such a love affair, even with the divine Son of God, has to be mutual. When we hear the call to discipleship, we face these questions: What about the image God has of me? Can God love me as I yearn to be loved? What is God's attitude when he looks at me? In the next chapter, we need to explore further how we see ourselves in God's sight.

chapter 2

What Are We Like for God?

*N*ow that we have considered some true and false images we have of God, we find ourselves asking: Does God have an image for us? Actually, the scriptures give us many images that express how God sees us. One such image will help us greatly with our own images of God and of ourselves. Each year on February 2, the Feast of the Presentation of the Lord in the Temple, the church chooses a reading for Eucharist from the final chapter of the Old Testament, from the prophet Malachi:

> Lo, I am sending my messenger
>
> > to prepare the way before me;
>
> And suddenly there will come to the temple
>
> > the LORD whom you seek,
>
> And the messenger of the covenant whom you
> > desire.

Yes, he is coming, says the LORD of hosts.

But who will endure the day of his coming?

And who can stand when he appears?

For he is like the refiner's fire,

or like the fuller's lye.

He will sit refining and purifying [silver],

and he will purify the sons of Levi,

Refining them like gold or like silver

that they may offer due sacrifice to the LORD.

—MALACHI 3:1–3

Lovers of Handel's *Messiah* will recognize this passage, but it is easy to miss its revelation of the way God sees us. The clue is "silver."

God's Silver

For the human race silver and gold are the romantic metals, the stuff of jewelry and heirlooms. Silver makes the ideal wedding gift, and it traditionally marks the twenty-fifth wedding anniversary. Mothers and grandmothers lovingly pass on their silver service to the next generations, who proudly display it and carefully insure it.

Practically speaking, humanity's love affair with silver doesn't make much sense. Stainless steel is practical; sterling silver is not. Silver tarnishes, turns ugly, and it must be polished, a messy and tedious process. Once polished, silver tarnishes again and again, year after year, generation after generation.

Still those mothers and grandmothers keep polishing the silver and keep on bequeathing it to loved ones. No one even considers bequeathing stainless steel to the youngsters. Why? Well, because stainless steel is a bit dull, and it's only stainless steel. And silver does look so beautiful when it's polished. Also, because the silver has been in the family ever so long. Finally, just because.

The truth is this: We are God's silver. All of us. God "sits refining and purifying" us all, his children, generation after generation, because he loves us. He knows that it is in our nature to become tarnished, to behave sinfully and ignore him, and that he must constantly call us back to himself and polish us with his attentive love and grace. God knows that we will go on getting more or less tarnished, and he will have to continue polishing. Even after Jesus Christ has "refined" us sacramentally through the power of his saving action, we will need that polishing all our lives long.

Why does God do it? He polishes us because he cherishes us. We are precious and valuable to him. He could have created a stainless-steel equivalent, but he created us. The reason why is a mystery, but the cherishing is real. The preaching of Jesus Christ is full of the good news of that cherishing.

This realization can calm our anxiety about our worth in God's eyes. It should not tempt us to complacency. After all, analogies limp, and we are not metal, but free women and men who can make graced choices either to tarnish or to be polished in God's sight. With his grace we can be "self-polishing" as silver never can. The important lesson this image teaches is that we are simultaneously cherished and imperfect. To God, "cherished" matters much more than "imperfect," and so it should matter much more to us.

Pause & Pray

Romans 1:15–8:1 The struggle within us between sinfulness and grace.

2 Corinthians 12:7–10 Living with human weakness year in and year out, with God's grace.

Does God Demand That We Be Perfect?

"How do I look? I must look awful. I feel awful. Tell me honestly, how bad do I look?" All of us have heard dialogue like that, at least in movies and on television. The scriptwriters had heard it before that, and suspected they could get a laugh of recognition from the audience.

That anxiety is merely in regard to physical appearance. What about how we come across to others as a whole person? What about how we come across to God? To ourselves? Is it more than a pretty thought that God could love us no matter what?

Some words of Jesus from the Sermon on the Mount have been so misinterpreted that they can be used to induce a neurotic, doomed perfectionism about ourselves. Ironically, these same words contain the truth than can free us from that perfectionism:

> But I say to you, love your enemies, and pray for those who persecute you, that you may be children of your heavenly Father, for he makes his sun rise on the bad and the good, and causes rain to fall on the just and the unjust. For if you love those who love you, what recompense will you have? Do not the tax collectors do the same? And if you greet your brothers only, what is

34

unusual about that? Do not the pagans do the same? So be perfect, just as your heavenly Father is perfect.

—MATTHEW 5:44–48

Many people hear those words as a discouraging call to perfection, but Jesus is teaching forgiveness, reconciliation, and spiritual growth here, and his teaching is based on the model of divine love. He is saying no to perfectionism and yes to our goodness as we are, even as he invites us to become more like him.

The model of love Christ gives us is his heavenly Father, who is inclusive and all-embracing in his love, not selective and discriminatory. What folly to believe that the sun shines and the rains fall only on good farmers' fields and that financial or agricultural failure is a sure sign of divine condemnation.

Still, many of us persist in believing that lie. In times of trouble we ask, "Why has God done this to me?" Rabbi Harold Kushner's book, *When Bad Things Happen to Good People,* explored just this subject—the mystery of divine love and human fate. We will return later to this mystery of fate and God's love for his human children, but the issue now is divine love and our images of ourselves.

Jesus teaches that the Father calls us to love each other and ourselves the way he does: with an unconditional, inclusive, all-embracing love. We are not permitted to draw up lists that include and exclude individuals or groups. We are to love God and to love our neighbors as ourselves—the two great commandments (Mark 12:28–31).

But there is a third commandment here, implicit in the second: We are to love ourselves, because that will be the yardstick for our love of others. No wonder we often treat others so shabbily—we have already treated ourselves the same way! Jesus, a supreme psychologist, demands that we learn from him to be gentle, accepting, and hopeful with ourselves, and then to turn to each other with that same gentleness, acceptance, and hope. This is the work of a lifetime: to be perfected in loving as our Father and Jesus love us, and as they teach us to love one other. It is the work of all our lifetimes, because it was first of all the lifework of Jesus—to bring us to this love.

We human children of the Father were alienated from him, from each other, and from ourselves. And still we are alienated, to greater or lesser degrees. Jesus is the bridge over this chasm of alienation, the loving Savior who heals and draws together the fractious people of God.

This image of Jesus can seem too good to be true, too idealistic to square with our own discouraging experience of ourselves. Sometimes we admit that it may be true for some people, but we still assume it can't be true for us. It's all very well to say that God wants us to love ourselves with as much acceptance and perseverance as he does, and to love each other that way too, to say that God wishes to perfect us in loving rather than in a kind of spiritual spotlessness. But how can that be? Just look at us!

Pause & Pray

Colossians 3:18–21 and *Ephesians 5:21–6:4* These Christian ideals for family relationships are the work of a lifetime! Every year the Colossians passage is read on the Feast of the Holy Family. (I have nicknamed this feast "sore-rib Sunday," after watching family members in the pews punch each other at pertinent moments.)

Colossians 3:1–17 The disciple's call to practice virtue and avoid sin is lifelong, and impossible without life in Christ.

The "Second Man"

Where does that voice come from within us, the voice that says, "How can God love me? Look at me!"? The American playwright S. N. Behrman explained the title of his play *The Second Man* by quoting from a letter of Lord Frederick Leighton, a famous and successful nineteenth-century British painter who may well have known that he and his work were overrated: "There is always that other strange second man in me, calm, critical, observant, unmoved, blasé, odious. . . ." How well that describes a great part of the problem with images of self: we are divided selves, with plural dimensions in our personalities. One of them, in so many of us, is the embryonic cynic.

The "second man"—what an accurate description of the voice within us that says to the offer of divine or human love, "Hold back," that says to forgiveness and reconciliation, "Not for you," that says to goodness and growth in ourselves or others, "Don't trust it."

How diabolical that voice is. Recall the voice of Screwtape, the senior devil in C. S. Lewis's *The Screwtape Letters*, and then look again at Leighton's list of adjectives: "calm, critical, observant, unmoved, blasé, odious." Do those words describe something within us that is savvy, cool, with-it, aware, and definitely no pushover? Do they recall the devil's voice, trying to kill now and forever all that could warm us to divine and human love?

Often we need to say no, a resolute no, to the coolest voice within us, especially when it urges us not to trust or respond to God's action in our lives. This "second man" or "second woman" is our spiritual enemy, especially in our efforts to believe and hope in God's acceptance and forgiveness of us.

There is a gospel version of this "second man" image. The parable of the prodigal son (Luke 15:11–32) has been called the best and most familiar short story in the Western world, and it may be the best-known of the parables of Jesus. However, I'm not sure how well people really know this story in its entirety. For instance, if we were to stop a hundred Christians on the street and ask them the to tell the story, I'm willing to bet many of them would get it wrong. If we asked them how the story ends, many might say, "Oh, that's easy. The son is a sinner, he has a change of heart and returns to his father, and his father forgives him and welcomes him back. A beautiful story."

Yes, all that happens, and it is a beautiful story, but the answer is wrong. Jesus' story of the prodigal son does not end with "happily ever after." It ends with a question mark. When we last hear of him, the father is out in the field, trying to persuade his angry, judgmental, older son to come in to the welcome-home party for his younger brother. And Jesus does not tell us whether or not the older brother finally comes to the party.

So much for a sweet, sentimental story with all the loose ends neatly tied up. In fact, the story of the prodigal son begins much more harshly than many of us realize. The crowd that heard the story for the first time would have noticed that. Jesus tells us that the younger son goes to his father and demands that he be given his inheritance immediately. In Israel at the time of Jesus, the elder son would have received two-thirds of his father's estate, and the younger son one-third. They both received their shares after their father's death. So the younger son is actually saying something like this to his father: "I'm bored out of my mind. I can't wait around for you to die. That could take years. Let's pretend you're dead now, and I'll take my share."

So far it's not a very sentimental story. Still, the father loves his son, and he gives him his share of the estate. The boy squanders it all and ends up feeding a rich man's pigs. One could not sink any lower in Jewish imagination, inasmuch as pigs were seen as the most unclean of animals, unfit for human consumption.

Jesus tells us that the young man "comes to his senses" and returns to his father, who has never stopped loving him and watching for him. The father sees him coming "from a long way off." He embraces his son and begins to give the servants orders to restore him to his former status: a robe, a ring, shoes for his feet. His father doesn't even pay attention to the son's little set speech about wanting to be only a servant now on the family farm. One is reminded of the person who asked Abraham Lincoln during the Civil War how he would deal with the Southern states after the war was over. Lincoln replied, "I will treat them as if they had never been away."

In contrast with his father, the prodigal son's older brother questions the judgment of his father in a self-righteous manner. This older brother is an unhappy, resentful man, as judgmental people often are. He is just angry enough to tell his father how he sees his own life on the farm as a grim round of duties. He also shows his complete lack of sympathy for his brother, whom he refers to as "your son." The older son also has a nasty mind; he imagines that his brother has wasted the money "with prostitutes."

One of the most important lessons of this story of the prodigal son is that each of us has within us a share of those two brothers. We are all sinners, like the younger son. We are also, in part, the older son: we sum up and write off others for their sins and failings. We resent God because we think he has treated his other children better. Moreover, the judgmental older son inside us can turn on the younger son within and say something like this: "You're disgusting. You'll never get any better. Do you think God can love or forgive you, the way you are? Forget it!" That's definitely what the voice of the "second man" sounds like.

Imagine how this story of the prodigal son might have turned out if the older brother had spotted his brother before his father did, about a mile up the road. We might never have had the reunion and the forgiveness. Perhaps that interior version of the story happens often, and many a Catholic never gets to confession because the older son within sneers, "Forget it. You could never be forgiven."

So the story of the prodigal son has no neat ending. It just stops. It's up to us to write our own ending. Will the younger son or daughter within each of us come home to the loving Father? Will the harsh older son or daughter come in to the welcome-home party of hope and forgiveness? The story is familiar, but we still get to choose the ending.

Pause & Pray

Luke 15:1–3, 11–32 Jesus responds to the intolerance of the Pharisees with the parable of the prodigal son.

Baskin-Robbins Spirituality
and the 491st Sin

We are not as forgiving of ourselves or of others as God is because we do not love ourselves or each other as unconditionally as he does. So we give up on ourselves much more readily. How often we have heard someone say, "What's the use of going to confession regularly? I end up telling the same sins over and over again." I think of that attitude as "Baskin-Robbins spirituality": we want to be truly original, inventive, interesting, and complicated penitents, with great variety from confession to confession. Perhaps we will come up with the "sin of the month," like the ice-cream store: "If this is August, it must be grand theft auto."

40

If that attitude does not exasperate a forgiving God, it has to sadden him. Of course we commit mostly the same sins, time after time; we are mostly the same persons. But only "mostly." If we trust in God's grace, he can help us to change and grow, to become less lazy, or gossipy, or selfish.

Character is not fate, and Jesus is Lord. By the power of his death and resurrection we have his life and the forgiveness of our sins. We need enough humility to accept ourselves as we are, just as God accepts us. As we continue our striving for holiness, we can feel much more joyful about the invitation to intimacy with God than we feel disappointed by how unready we are. Hope can overcome our discouraged pride and spiritual fastidiousness.

One problem with trusting in God's forgiveness is our own vindictive streak. Peter asked Jesus a question most of us have thought about: "Lord, if my brother sins against me, how often must I forgive him? As many as seven times?" The apostle fed Jesus what he considered a generous suggestion: seven times. Jesus, hinting at God's boundless love, responded with "seventy-seven times" (Matthew 18:21–22).

That answer reminds me of my favorite single moment in *Wuthering Heights*. Though I may roast in literary hell for this, it is a moment of humor! To be exact, it is a throwaway, anticlerical one-liner by Emily Brontë, a clergyman's daughter. Early in the novel, Mr. Lockwood, the new tenant at Thrushcross Grange, is spending a cold night as the unwelcome guest of Heathcliff at Wuthering Heights. In the spare bedroom, Lockwood finds a volume of collected sermons. He nods off after reading the title of one sermon: "Seventy Times Seven, and the First of the Seventy-First."

Think of it, the 491st sin. Someone had bothered to multiply seventy times seven and come up with 490.

From there it's only a short step to picturing God in our own human image, waiting for the very next sin, the fatal 491st. Now he can pounce on the hapless sinner, shouting, "Gotcha!" How human, how literal, and how absurd. We are called to change our human way of judging to resemble more closely the divine way, not to imagine divine judgment as a human narrow-mindedness writ large across the sky.

Another problem with understanding and accepting divine forgiveness is our tendency to apply a worldly model of success and failure to sin and forgiveness. The kingdom of heaven has a different set of values, expressed in the Beatitudes. Those values are quite at variance with the world's values. On Wall Street, along the Potomac, and on Main Street as well, the meek, the sorrowing, and the poor are not regarded as blessed.

Keeping score and measuring ourselves with lists of successes and failures are not the way of Jesus Christ, who told us the story of the prodigal son. Christ doesn't call his disciples to be successful, only to be committed and faithful, and, when necessary, repentant. We Christians are inclined to call ourselves to "success" in virtue and then to give up when we don't achieve a perfect score.

Yet our sense of being "God's silver" can help us to realize that we are simultaneously cherished and imperfect. Here is another image that can reinforce this: Picture a large fruit tree near a house. Its beauty delights the eye. Its fruit is delicious. Its leaves give welcome shade. Still, those same leaves die and fall to the ground, creating a mess, a nuisance, an eyesore, and much work for someone. Most of us accept the "package" of fruit, shade, beauty, and leaves on the ground. Instinctively we flinch from the argument that says, "Just chop the thing down, then your problem is gone." Yes, but then the shade, the fruit, and the beauty are gone too. We'll keep the tree, and we'll learn something about God's having us in his keeping.

Pause & Pray

Matthew 13:24–30 Consider God's patience with good and evil, sin and virtue existing alongside each other in the church. Can God's grace transform weeds into wheat as growth takes place?

Earthen Vessels

Saint Paul gives us one of the most profound images of this paradox of God's cherishing us in the midst of our imperfection:

> For God who said, "Let light shine out of darkness," has shone in our hearts to bring to light the knowledge of the glory of God on the face of [Jesus] Christ. But we hold this treasure in earthen vessels, that the surpassing power may be of God and not from us.
>
> —2CORINTHIANS 4:6–7

Again, the positive gift of being a "vessel" is conditioned by being "earthen." But our call to be filled with the light of God in Christ is so much more important than our fragility, vulnerability, and imperfection as mortal, sinful women and men. While the word "earthen" conditions "vessel," and makes grace so crucial, it is our vesselhood that can transform our earthenness, and gloriously so, as it has done in God's saints, both canonized and uncanonized.

The silver, the tree, the fragile vessel—all these images speak of God's vision of us, not in spite of our limitations and weaknesses but in the midst of them, accepting and working with them. God's love teaches us to accept our flaws as inseparable dimensions of ourselves. They are conditions of our existence, not evil stains to be removed before we can appear before the loving Lord or accept ourselves.

The image of an earthen vessel serves as a powerfully honest way of seeing leadership in the church. Too often in the past the dominant image of the church seemed to be the *Wagon Train* model, with the leader as the wagon master. I am referring to a weekly program from the days of "paleo-TV." Most television viewers of a certain age remember the popular series starring Ward Bond as the wagon master. Every week this square-jawed, omni-competent, well-seasoned hero led a group of neurotic nineteenth-century greenhorns across the barren wastes, past countless dangers into the promised land out west. The wagon master knew every rock, bush, tree, mountain, river, desert, arrowhead, and hostile tribe. Nothing fazed him. He was a superior know-it-all. He'd been there before, countless times. There were no surprises for him.

That is not the New Testament image of leadership, because it does not square with Saint Paul's image of all of us Christians, leaders included, as earthen vessels. Even though some of us are called to serve as guides and leaders for others, there is still a crucial difference between the wagon master and us: this journey through the Christian life is the first and only trip for all of us, leaders included. In many situations we are greenhorns as well. All church members need to realize that the Christian pilgrimage is not *Wagon Train*, and that leaders and those they lead learn and grow along the way, led by the Holy Spirit, who alone is all-wise.

Another way of looking at our situation might be through the image of the construction site. Even though there are signs of progress, construction sites bother us in some ways. Someone who has toured a home or office during a building project has heard the litany of apologies throughout. It sounded like this: "Well, you can't see it very well with everything in a mess like this, but it will look great once the carpeting is down, and the windows are in, and all that stuff over there has been cleaned out. You should come back a month from now when the decorating is done." There's a lesson for disciples in that experience. We need to make peace with the fact that all Christians, including their spiritual leaders, are God's construction sites: developing, incomplete, and messy for as long as life goes on. For what it's worth, the church is a construction site as well—the grandest, and sometimes the messiest, of all.

If each of us is God's construction site, it stands to reason that he transforms us gradually, over a lifetime. However, God's grace of conversion can also work rapidly and dramatically. We often pass actual construction sites where we see no progress for a long time, then suddenly we notice that much has been accomplished. Such growth is also possible in the Christian life.

In his commentary on the New Testament, Dr. William Barclay tells a fine story about a workman in London who went to a pub every evening with his friends and drank away his earnings. As a result his wife and children were near starvation, living in squalor.

One day the workman went to a temperance meeting, stopped drinking, and became a churchgoer. His drinking buddies were annoyed at the loss of their mate, so they taunted him mercilessly about his newfound faith in Jesus Christ. One fellow asked him, "Do you really believe that Christ turned water into wine?" The workman replied, "I don't know about that, but you can come over to my house and see how he turned beer into furniture."

We need to pray for miracles of grace, and open our lives to them. They are not inconsistent with our being lifelong construction sites. As Flannery O'Connor said, those who don't need a Savior can't have one. We should ask ourselves: What is the "beer" in our life that the Spirit of Christ can transform into "furniture"?

Jesus Searches the Margins

Is there any point in asking how the Father sees us? How can we know the mind of God? It is true that we cannot know what God knows, or see what he sees; but we can believe in what he reveals, what he chooses to tell us through Jesus Christ, his Word made flesh. How Jesus talks about and treats people is a revelation of what God sees in them. When we listen to the familiar stories of the prodigal son or the good Samaritan, we need to feel the prickly human sensation of overhearing someone talking about us.

What we will hear is that Jesus has a peculiar preference for the outsider, the sinner, the person on the margin of society and life. And so does his Father. We need to let Christ speak through these parables to the sinner and outsider in each of us.

Zacchaeus is an excellent example of this divine passion (Luke 19:1–10). The little extortionist climbs a tree to get a better look at the Galilean preacher. Jesus calls up to him to come down, because he is to host Jesus at his house for a meal. The good people of the town are shocked, but Zacchaeus expresses his change of heart by promising to become just and generous in his new life. Jesus in turn says that salvation has come to the house of Zacchaeus this day. Zacchaeus is not a one-time exception, but exactly the kind of "lost" person Jesus was sent to seek out.

The little tax collector was probably restless and dissatisfied with his life, on the lookout (literally) for something or someone to open him up to a life of love and meaning. Like Matthew, another tax collector,

Zacchaeus was a prime candidate for meeting Jesus Christ and letting him change his life. A self-righteous person, full of self, is much less open to conversion than is a hungry seeker. The outsider yearns for a justice and love that the world does not give.

Is this too optimistic an interpretation of how God sees us as yearning sinners? Does it ignore or downplay God's justice and our own call to live virtuously? As I consider those questions, I am reminded of a Christmas card I received many years ago. I still have it. The card had no evident religious theme. Instead, it was a *comic* Christmas card! It was the sort of thing one priest might send to another as a joke. (One did.)

The front of the card shows a large Christmas tree, and four sentences are printed in black over the tree: "Some people say they're messy. Some people say they're a fire hazard. Some people say they ruin the carpet. Some people say they can never get them to look right." Inside, the card reads: "But I say they're my relatives and they're coming over for Christmas."

That's it! Not romantic, or optimistic, or fuzzy-minded, just realistic. We are God's relatives and he has us over for Christmas, and every day, if we will trust him and show up. We are messy in so many ways. We have always been a fire hazard. Since Hiroshima and Nagasaki we have been so in apocalyptic proportions. We do go on ruining the carpet of the planet God created, and many of the other furnishings as well. We can never get ourselves or each other to look right, especially if "look right" is a code phrase for being perfect. Nonetheless, the Father loves us as we are and for what we can become, and for what we have already become in his Son.

The Father loves us, and he wants us to stop flogging each other and ourselves with false expectations that tempt us to give up. God does have expectations of us, but they sound so different from what we often imagine.

We can hear Jesus saying just that in the poignant invitation at the end of Matthew's eleventh chapter: "Come to me, all you who labor and are burdened, and I will give you rest. Take my yoke upon you and learn from me, for I am meek and humble of heart; and you will find rest for yourselves. For my yoke is easy, and my burden light" (Matthew 11:28–30).

Pause & Pray

2 Corinthians 1:8–11 St. Paul exhorts us to keep faith and hope alive in the midst of our trials. Are there present struggles in my life to which Christ addresses these words?

Luke 19:1–10 Zacchaeus the tax collector doesn't yet "look right" to the townspeople, but Jesus is delighted with him. How does that speak to my self-perception?

"What Will Everyone Think?"

Even if we do begin to concede that God loves us in the midst of our faults, we can still dread the judgment of our families, friends, and others. We've had too many experiences that told us firsthand about the poor images others had of us. These memories are so strong that, even when we are complimented or affirmed, that voice of the "second man" within us can be heard to say, "Yes, but if they knew me as I really am, with all my secret temptations and fantasies, my yearnings and my sins, how I would disgust them!"

Such experiences and such a voice have done much to lower us in our own estimation, and have contributed to our sense of God's disappointment with us. Indeed, that voice within could go on to press the point: "If all those other people would be disgusted, just think about God—he knows all your secrets!"

That voice is as false as it is evil. For proof of that, think about an experience most of us have had: a friend or relative has trusted us enough to say that he or she needed to talk to us about something very serious and confidential that we must not reveal to anyone. Then that person has told us of some embarrassing sin or failing, often with feelings of shame and self-rejection. We listened to that friend or relative, and tried to be consoling. Then eventually we parted for a while.

Here's the interesting part: How did we feel immediately after the other person's self-revelation? What did we say to ourselves? Was it something like this: "How disgusting! To think that I ever associated with scum like that! I feel as if I need a shower!"? That's very unlikely. On the contrary, we probably never before felt as close to that person as we did right after our conversation. We respected and loved that person perhaps more than ever, and felt deeply committed to his or her healing and welfare.

Isn't that intriguing in the light of what the "second man" voice says to us? Isn't it a curious chemistry of human love and relationships that we often respond most lovingly to people when they are most vulnerable and needy? Of course there are exceptions, but I'm describing us in our best and most loving moments. What's more, aren't those the very moments during which we most resemble the loving God in whose image we are made?

If we sinners can show love and acceptance to others who need it, we can be sure of the Father's unfailing love, without exceptions and failures. In relating to a sinner, God is very much like a mother with a sick child, who gets all the more focus and attention for being weak and in need. That's why the shepherd leaves the ninety-nine and goes in search of the one lost sheep. God will never be outdone by human generosity. Jesus says a direct no to such a fear when he describes the Father in this fashion:

> "For everyone who asks, receives; and the one who seeks, finds; and to the one who knocks, the door will be opened. What father among you would hand his son a snake when he asks for a fish? Or hand him a scorpion when he asks for an egg? If you then, who are wicked, know how to give good gifts to your children, how much more will the Father in heaven give the holy Spirit to those who ask him?".
>
> —LUKE 11:10–13

It is hard for us to trust God's love enough to ask him for the Holy Spirit, that is, for whatever his love wants to give us, and for the grace to respond to it, so that we can become more and more one with him. That sounds risky, and it can make us fearful.

Perfect love drives out fear (1 John 4:18), and knowing that the kingdom of God is a conspiracy of love goes a long way toward scattering the darkness of our suspicions, distrust, and fear. God's love for us is perfect, and our love for him is not. There is some admixture of fear, but only one kind of "fear of the Lord" is worthy of a Christian spiritual life: the fear of offending the Beloved.

Human friends and lovers know that the fear of offending someone they love is no weak, negligible experience. How the human heart can suffer, fearing that a loved one has been offended, or even misunderstood or ignored! By the same token, for the committed and sensitive Christian who loves the Lord, the fear of the "Hurler into Hell" is less fierce than the loving fear of having failed the Crucified and Risen One. Loving fear draws us to reconciliation and forgiveness, to begin again with the Lord of new beginnings.

chapter 3

What Is God's Plan For Us?

*L*et's think back over those questions I considered when we began to look at images for disciples. We have heard the Christian gospel offer joyous answers to several of them: God is a good and loving Father, offering unconditional love, forgiveness, and eternal life through his Son, Jesus. And he does all this because he sees us as good, deserving of his love, and precious in his eyes, though far from perfect.

But many questions about our life in the Spirit remain. In human relationships we know that two good people might be friends but that doesn't mean they actually are friends. And even if they have been friends, couldn't they misunderstand each other, have conflicting expectations of the friendship, or grow gradually apart from each other? And what if times turn bad? In the heart of the marriage vows a man and a woman use such phrases as "for richer, for poorer; in sickness and in health." Is there a version of those promises that exists between God and his human children?

When we apply such questions to an intimate relationship between God and a human person, the questions seem to increase. How can there be understanding and intimacy between an invisible God and a "mere mortal"? Isn't such a relationship even more impossible than trying to make a two-year-old and an adult best friends? Not really. If Jesus, the Father's divine Son, could make the first disciples his friends and the Father's, he can do the same for all of us.

Still, the larger question remains: How do things really stand between this loving God and ourselves? We can begin our search for an answer when we admit what we don't know. We don't know ourselves, each other, or God. That is, we don't know any of these persons the way we know maps, multiplication tables, or chemical formulas. Each human heart is a mystery, and certainly God is mystery, in a philosopher's sense of mystery: not a problem to be solved but a mystery to be lived. A problem is something we have, like a flat tire or a toothache. A mystery is something that has us; it is bigger than we are and takes us in—like falling in love.

When we don't know the answer to a question about God, it is tempting to make one up. That's a temptation we need to resist. Just to live for a while with a question about God, perhaps for a long while, is not so appealing, but it is the healthier and more honest course.

Pause & Pray

Job 40:1–14; 42:1–6 I cannot have a "God's-eye" view of my life or of the world. How does this truth challenge me to faith and to hope?

Matthew 11:25–27 Jesus Christ shows me all I can know about God, and that can give me peace—if I let it.

What About Suffering?

Our relationship with God is unique. He's not our supervisor or our foreman. God is our creator. Of course, statements exactly like that one have scared some of us away from closeness with God in the past. But we realize from what he has revealed that God is a loving creator, unconditionally committed to an eternal love affair with us through the humanity and divinity of his Son. Still, trust comes hard for us, because we can't understand God, we can't "take him in," as he can take us into himself. So a voice within us, perhaps that "second man" voice, will demand a guarantee from God, some way of being certain that, no matter what, he will not change toward us. And, as proof of God's guaranteed love, we insist that no evil befall us once we are his.

But that is not the good news of the kingdom of God. This insistence on a guarantee from God is best described in a deservedly famous passage from the Gifford Lectures (1953–54) of the theologian John Macmurray:

> The maxim of illusory religion runs: "Fear not; trust in God and he will see that none of the things you fear will happen to you"; that of real religion, on the contrary, is: "Fear not; the things you are afraid of are quite likely to happen to you, but they are nothing to be afraid of."[1]

We need to look at the life of Jesus closely. He loved the Father, and he claimed that the Father loved him. What proved the Father's love for Jesus? Was it his Son's incredible, lifelong good luck? His freedom from any kind of pain or suffering? Was it Jesus' dying in bed, surrounded by loved ones, at an advanced old age? Hardly. Jesus lived a life of love and sacrifice because of his and the Father's love for us. It was a life worth living. His Father's perfect love for Jesus, his perfect presence and faithfulness to him, made Jesus certain and fearless in his loving service to the Father and us. In his perfect faithfulness, the Father raised Jesus from the dead.

That's what Jesus came to share with us as the adult children of God: not a pain-free, trouble-free existence, but the love of the Father that overcomes fear and sin, pain and death. Perfect love does cast out fear, but it doesn't anesthetize against suffering. Without the paralysis of fear, however, we can walk throughout our lives with Jesus into the Father's eternal embrace.

Jesus did not want to suffer, nor did the Father want him to suffer, but both of them loved us enough to permit all that suffering for the sake of our salvation. And it is their loving will that we too struggle against suffering, and relieve the sufferings of our brothers and sisters as much as possible. We are called to continue the healing compassion of Christ in the world.

But that's not good enough for the "second man" in us. That ungraced voice applies the pleasure-pain principle to God's dealings with us, and God is found wanting. He's not loving enough or powerful enough to protect us from suffering. And protecting us from suffering becomes the pass-fail test for any self-respecting god.

Which is a bit like saying: "I don't care if God made me his cherished silver. Couldn't he have made me stainless steel? It's so much easier and more enjoyable to be stainless steel." And God understands our crying out against the conditions of our life. It is for us to understand that our vision of them is only partial and that this partial vision makes us resentful.

God did not make us other gods. The Creator made us creatures. God is eternal; we are mortal. He is powerful; we are vulnerable. God is infinite; we are limited. On and on the contrasts go.

This all-too-human dissatisfaction reminds me of the story of my third Christmas. Fortunately, I was too young to remember it, but my parents delighted in telling the story, especially in front of me.

I was an only child, but throughout December my mother and father took me from toy department to toy department, covering most of the stores in the city. On Christmas morning, I was led into our small living room, jammed full of all the delights that could be purchased on the salary of an assistant cashier in a bank during the late 1930s. True love and scrimping had made that quite a lot. I took a long look around, and then said, "Where is everything else?" (And that was a couple of decades before Peggy Lee sang "Is That All There Is?")

Of course, the point is not that we are stuck with a minor deity, a kind of assistant cashier among gods. Rather, God is boundlessly great and loving; he has made us for himself; we have a life (ultimately, a perfect, eternal one) that has its limitations and imperfections now (built into our creaturehood). We need to be grateful and get on with living our lives in the grace of a loving God.

Pause & Pray

John 15:18–21 Jesus warns us: his followers will be treated as he was. That happens to us individually and together as church. How do I respond when it happens?

Acts 9:15–16 Witnessing to Jesus will involve us in his suffering.

Is Christian Stoicism the Answer?

The uncompromising call of Jesus to his followers to pick up their crosses daily and follow him is not to be interpreted as a call for Christian stoicism. Jesus said that he had compassion on the crowds who brought him their sufferings, and he proved it by never turning them away, by always healing the sick in answer to their pleas and expressions of faith. Even the doubtful and uncertain were brought along by his challenge to have faith, to which at least one responded, "I do believe, help my unbelief!" (Mark 9:24). When Jesus hesitated to help the Syrophoenician woman, telling her that it was not right to take the food of sons and daughters and throw it to the dogs, she answered that even the dogs eat the leavings that fall from their masters' tables. Marveling at her faith, Jesus healed her daughter from afar (Mark 7:24–30).

We do not have a divine judge and savior who calls us to a cold, bloodless effort to repress all feelings and make ourselves indifferent to pleasure or pain, to grief or joy. Instead, we have Jesus Christ, who expressed his agony in the garden, who died, nailed to a tree, crying out to his Father. He endured all of that so that we, united with him by grace, might walk through the perils of this imperfect life to the joy and glory of eternal union. That plan of salvation is as far from stoicism as a love letter is from a No Trespassing sign.

Pause & Pray

John 11:21–44 Divine power in Jesus raises Lazarus from the dead, but human emotions cause him to weep for his friends.

Romans 12:9–15 How our human feelings and our efforts can respond to Christ's call.

Is Suffering a Punishment for Sin?

As early as our discussion of "Gawd" in the first chapter, we touched on the perennial urge of many believers to blame human suffering on God and to explain it as his direct and personalized punishment for sin. This superstition is common to religions around the world and throughout history, Judaism and Christianity not excepted. This particular tenet gets packaged and explained in various ways. Basically, though, those who hold it contend that "Gawd" keeps score of our sins and gets even by sending individual suffering flying in our direction, often with no apparent matching of the severity of the punishment to the presumed offense.

Jesus did address this error head-on, and his words demand careful interpretation:

> At that time some people who were present there told him about the Galileans whose blood Pilate had mingled with the blood of their sacrifices. He said to them in reply, "Do you think that because these Galileans suffered in this way they were greater sinners than all other Galileans? By no means! But I tell you, if you do not repent, you will all perish as they did! Or those eighteen people who were killed when the tower at Siloam fell on them—do you think they

were more guilty than everyone else who lived in Jerusalem? By no means! But I tell you, if you do not repent, you will all perish as they did!".

—LUKE 13:1–5

Jesus clearly establishes that swords don't strike people and towers don't collapse on them because God can't abide their sinfulness a moment longer. There is just no such connection, Jesus says, so stop making one: and especially stop remaking your image of God to fit such vengeful behavior. According to Jesus Christ, his Father does not play a lethal kind of dodge ball with his human children: "By no means! . . . By no means!"

In that same passage from Luke, though, Jesus twice adds a strong warning: "But I tell you, you will all come to the same end unless you reform." It's not a threat but an honest statement of the way of human life and salvation. We know that our sinfulness—addiction, selfishness, violence—can hasten our own deaths and those of others. Death also is an effect of original sin. Our call as disciples is to repentance for our sins, renewal of our lives, and readiness for judgment and eternal life, whenever that comes. And it can come suddenly and unexpectedly, so we need to be prepared. But that is a very different message from declaring suffering and death in individual instances to be punishments for individual sinfulness.

Physical death is one kind of death, but there is another. Saint John speaks of "second death," the eternal banishment to hell, everlasting separation from the face of God in heaven (Revelation 20:6 and 21:8). In order to live eternal life with Jesus Christ we need to repent and believe the good news. We need to live out the good news in our daily lives; otherwise we will die spiritually as surely as everyone dies physically. And if a loving God uses human circumstances in his polishing and refining of his beloved silver, that is a very different activity from celestial dart throwing.

58

Pause & Pray

Luke 13:1–5 Jesus definitively breaks the link between sin and human suffering. Am I able to do that?

Psalm 32 Suffering often accompanies sin not as a divine thunderbolt but as a natural effect.

"Be More Like Your Brother"

Jesus teaches us clearly what it means for us to be his brothers and sisters in the family of God, in the kingdom of heaven. He describes carefully the challenge and the reward of being an adult child of God, not a two-year-old trying to relate to an adult. At a critical moment in Mark's gospel the whole relationship is laid out for us. Jesus has just predicted for the first time that he will suffer, be put to death, and be raised up by the Father on the third day. Peter then urges Jesus not to talk like that. Sternly, Jesus warns Peter not to deny or avoid the paschal mystery, the death and resurrection of the Messiah. Then, turning to the whole crowd, including all of us, he says:

> "Whoever wishes to come after me must deny himself, take up his cross, and follow me. For whoever wishes to save his life will lose it, but whoever loses his life for my sake and that of the gospel will save it. What profit is there for one to gain the whole world and forfeit his life? What could one give in exchange for his life? Whoever is ashamed of me and of my words in this faithless and sinful generation, the Son of Man will be ashamed of when he comes in his Father's glory with the holy angels."
>
> —MARK 8:34–38

The cross of Jesus is at the heart of our relationship with him and with the Father. It is the cross of our daily struggles as well as the cross as the symbol of death, Christ's and ours, and of resurrection, his and ours. We are as intimately joined to Jesus as branches to a vine; if the vine suffered for his fidelity to his father's will, then so will the branches. But if his Father companioned Jesus through that suffering and raised him to eternal glory, he will do the same for us. And the life-and-death struggle is even more a spiritual reality than it is a physical one, though it is both.

At the heart of the mystery of Christ is a radical contradiction of all our normal human calculations and assumptions. Uncompromisingly, Jesus asserts that this life on earth is not all that matters. He teaches that we are not all alone in our struggles; that we ought not to put ourselves first in every instance; that pain, poverty, suffering, sorrow, weakness, and death are not the worst things that can happen to us.

What does matter most? Jesus teaches that what we must preserve at all costs is our life in God. This is why we were created: to live here and forever in the kingdom of heaven. If we lose the self that we were made to be and called to become in him, then all is lost. Even if we trade that God-centered self for the whole world, all is lost. If we lose all that we could have achieved, all that we have made of ourselves on our own, but do not lose the God-centered self, then nothing that matters is lost. So the only way to make sure that we do become that God-centered self is to follow Christ and to imitate him all our lives long, especially in the carrying of our crosses, especially in the matter of loving and losing.

No child likes to hear a parent say, "I wish you were more like your brother." How that grates on us! But God does call us to become more like Jesus while remaining ourselves. The Father does this not to put us down but to unite us more closely to the one who died and rose for us.

That call gives us a strange litmus test for our following of Jesus. There are two nearly infallible signs that we are living the Christian life: if we are always in love and always in trouble! Why? Because that's how Jesus lived. Of course, that kind of living makes discernment an important gift of the Spirit, because we constantly need to make sure that we are in the right kinds of love and the right kinds of trouble—Jesus' kinds.

Living a trouble-free existence was no proof of the Father's love for Jesus, and it is no proof of his love for us either. What counts is closeness to Jesus, to his life, his example, his teachings, his church, his sacraments. What's vital is Christ's presence to us in our prayer and in our sisters and brothers—that is proof that we are living the Christian life, and it is always accompanied by the struggles of Jesus as well, whatever particular forms they may take in each life.

Pause & Pray

John 12:24–26 The cost of discipleship is to be treated as Christ was.

2 Timothy 4:6–8 The struggles of the Christian life and its eternal reward.

Promises Versus Guarantees

That's how things stand between God and us. This "way things are" explains much about our attempts to deny, ignore, or resist it. For example, we so badly want a guarantee from Jesus for a trouble-free existence that we won't accept and cherish his promise to bring us personally to the Father. It doesn't occur to us that promises are for lovers and guarantees are for tire stores. No one receives a wedding announcement inviting them to be present on Saturday, the twenty-third, when Bob and Linda will exchange guarantees of marriage. No, vows and promises are for lovers who trust; guarantees are for strangers who do business together.

But is God trustworthy? Is he a "God of his word"? Not according to a lot of us Christians. For example, in the first chapter of the Acts of the Apostles, shortly before his ascension to the Father, Jesus hears the apostles ask him, "Lord, are you at this time going to restore the kingdom to Israel?" Jesus answers, "It is not for you to know the times or seasons that the Father has established by his own authority. But you will receive power when the holy Spirit comes upon you, and you will be my witnesses in Jerusalem, throughout Judea and Samaria, and to the ends of the earth" (Acts 1:6–8). Twenty centuries later Christians are still spilling barrels of ink on guessing games about the time of the end of the world, instead of getting on with evangelization and Christian living, which is what they have the Holy Spirit's power to do.

It is so difficult for us to trust Christ and to take him at his word. It's hard when his teaching goes against our expectations and desires, for example, regarding love and forgiveness of neighbor. The very trusting in itself is hard, because it demands that we believe unconditionally in his love for us and that we hope without wavering for him to deliver us. Letting go to the mysterious, paschal plan of God is critical, and we need to consider further our perennial struggle to preserve and to lose ourselves in the Lord's way, not in the world's.

There's a story that illustrates this need—and motive—for letting go to God. A distraught young woman, whose second child was stillborn and baptized conditionally, approached her elderly pastor. She was afraid that her child would never be with God in heaven. The pastor knew that she had one other child, a little boy. He listened to her agonizing doubts for a while and then asked her,

"Would you be willing to sacrifice the life of your little boy to be sure that your dead child is in heaven?" The woman was horrified. She said, "Father, what a terrible thing to say! How could you even ask that?" He responded, "You're right, it is terrible, for you and me. But it's true. It's a mystery, but it's true. God the Father did exactly what I asked you. He sent his only Son to die on the cross so that you and I and your little boy and your baby—and all people—could be with him in heaven. Aren't you glad that a God like that is going to decide the eternal life of your little baby, instead of people as unsure of themselves as you and I are?" As an instance of pastoral style it probably falls under the heading of "Shock Therapy," but the woman went home that night more at peace, and with a lesson about trust in God that she would not soon forget.

Of course, no amount of images or stories make our suffering painless, or even explain it. For Christian believers, suffering is a mystery, but it is not an absurdity. Its mystery has meaning, a meaning given it by Jesus Christ, who shared it with us, right up to, through, and beyond death, the worst that human suffering can do. For believer and unbeliever alike, the words of Emily Dickinson sound truly poignant: "Parting is all we know of heaven/and all we need of hell."[2] Poignant, yes; convincing, no. In Jesus Christ we are convinced that we know much, much more of heaven than any parting ever taught us. If the cross of Christ did not sum him up, and was not the end of him, then our crosses don't sum us up and aren't the end of us either.

"Yes, but what's the point of it all?" To do always the will of the Father, Jesus said. Doing the Father's loving, life-giving, and life-sacrificing will gave the whole meaning to Jesus' living and dying. That same will raised him to life on the third day and brought him to the Father's side forever, sending the Spirit of Love to do the same will among all the followers of Jesus until he comes again.

We meet many obstacles to doing God's will: our uncertainty about it, especially in detail; our weakness in facing its demands; the temptation to wander off, to just lie down for a while, or even for a lifetime. But one of the most difficult obstacles is the competition between the divine will and human planning. T. S. Eliot described modern men and women as "dreaming of systems so perfect that no one will need to be good."[3] How many examples we can bring forward for that. Politicians are always telling us that if only the government will get into everything or out of everything (depending on the party), then all will be well. If only we will adopt this program or abandon that one, we will be fine. If only we will return to the past or destroy every vestige of it, we will be saved. With good planning and careful editing and superior arrangements and truly enlightened selfishness, we can dispense with virtue and still achieve contentment.

Of course, none of it has worked. But we keep doggedly at it, like a motorist pumping and re-pumping air into the same flat tire. Trying to be good annoys and bores us; systems and programs fascinate us. It seems to me that the "sign of the secular Trinity" could be rendered: "In the name of Power, and of Control, and of the Long-Range Plan. Amen." Being "always in love and always in trouble" for Christ and his kingdom doesn't sound as appealing as being always in control. But it is truer to life, and much more nearly full of life.

Is God against planning then? Far from it. Salvation itself was carefully planned, as the opening verses of the Letter to the Ephesians make clear. But there are two kinds of planning, one deadly and one life-giving. We can find them both described in the Gospel of Luke, and in the same chapter (chapter 12). Jesus first tells the story of the rich man with the good harvest who planned his building and expansion program, then said to himself (the center of his life): "You have so many good things stored up for many years, rest, eat, drink, be merry!" But God said to him, "You fool! This night your life will be demanded of you; and the things you have prepared, to whom will they belong?" Jesus then makes this point: "Thus will it be for the one who stores up treasure for himself but is not rich in what matters to God" (Luke 12:16–21).

Well, if that kind of self-centered, selfish planning is deadly for the human spirit, what kind of planning works for Christians? Jesus teaches us the nature of Christian planning:

> "Do not be afraid any longer, little flock, for your Father is pleased to give you the kingdom. Sell your belongings and give alms. Provide money bags for yourselves that do not wear out, an inexhaustible treasure in heaven that no thief can reach nor moth destroy. For where your treasure is, there also will your heart be."
>
> —LUKE 12:32–34

Pause & Pray

Ephesians 1:3–10 Jesus Christ is God's plan of salvation.

So it's fine with God if we pile up treasure, as long as it is kingdom treasure. The keyword is "kingdom." Jesus is constantly contrasting the values of the world with those of the kingdom he has come to proclaim. We Christians may vote and pay taxes in a republic, but our allegiance is to a king, Christ the King. His values are ours, and we have already seen how different they are from those of the world around us. The spiritual values of the kingdom of God contradict the world's ideals of riches, success, fame, power, and the self always at the center of it all.

And, at first, the spiritual values of the kingdom are no match for the world's values. Saint Augustine had much experience in choosing worldly values and resisting spiritual ones, and there is great wisdom about these choices in his *Confessions*. That entire work seems to guide us toward this principle: material gifts, when we do not possess them, attract us, but when we do possess them, they do not satisfy us; spiritual gifts, when we do not possess them, do not attract us, but when we do possess them, they satisfy us. I believe Augustine is saying that the race between these two sets of values does not seem fair but that God has actually fixed the race in the Christian's favor. The tortoise of kingdom love and sacrifice always defeats the hare of worldly selfishness—but only by staying in the race until the end.

However, our zeal for the kingdom's values must not lead us to despise and distrust creation. Our faith is incarnational, and it does not reject the goods of this life as evil. When we go astray, the fault is not in the things among which we wander but in our choosing to wander. We are to use and enjoy all the rest of creation according to God's will for us. Anything or anyone who unites us more closely with the love of God and his service is good in his sight.

It's not necessary that something seem "holy" in a stained-glass sense. For instance, it is enough that some recreational activity relaxes us, renews us, and makes us more "alive"; in doing so, it contributes to our spiritual growth and health, and thus to our doing God's will. We do God's will when we choose to use our inner gifts and the things around us, and choose to relate to each other, in such a manner that we deepen the life of the kingdom within us and extend its influence among others. Things are not against God's will for us because they are evil; rather, they are evil only when our use of them is against God's will.

The three temptations of Christ in the desert illustrate this spiritual principle perfectly. Jesus did not say no to miraculous bread, a death-defying leap, and ruling the world because they were vicious or intrinsically evil. He said no because they were not the Father's loving will for him at that moment. They were not consistent with the divine plan for our salvation. That's precisely why the devil offered them to Jesus.

It is interesting to note that, later on, all three of these realities became the Father's will for his Son. Jesus fed thousands with miraculous bread, and then he himself became for all time the miraculous bread from heaven on our altars. Christ entered into Jerusalem and abandoned himself to the murderous plans of his enemies, and his Father raised him up. Now he is worshiped throughout the world as Christ the King. The issue was never "bad things." It was always the Father's will.

Jesus teaches by his words and his life that doing the Father's loving will fills us with his life here and leads us to the fullness of that life in eternal union with him. Resurrection, for Jesus and for us, is the core of Christian belief; it is the heart of the good news, and, along with the incarnation, the most controversial of all doctrines. The teaching that God's divine Son became man while remaining God and that he lived and died among us and was raised on the third day has been a scandal to Jews and an absurdity to Gentiles from the beginning (1 Corinthians 1:23). It still is. Christians are accused of going against all evidence of the senses and all reason, of countenancing injustice on earth with the promise of pie in the sky when they die, of despising the world that exists for the sake of a fantasy that most certainly does not. For our critics our belief in the paschal mystery of death and resurrection is, at best, self-delusion and, at worst, wrong-headed and dehumanizing for all who take it seriously.

Pause & Pray

Luke 4:1–13 The temptations of Christ were not necessarily temptations to bad things, but they were not the Father's loving will.

Matthew 26:36–46 Christ in the Garden of Gethsemane: Pray for what you will, but pray most of all for what the Father wills.

Is Every Believer Something of a Galileo?

"How can you say the dead rise?" Well, it's a matter of faith. But that question makes me think of sunrises and sunsets. Those are interesting words, "sunrise" and "sunset." For over three hundred years now, educated people have learned from Galileo and other astronomers that the earth revolves around the sun, not the other way around. Yet these same educated people will say such things to each other as, "Did you see that beautiful sunset last night?" or "What time is sunrise tomorrow?" They know that the sun does not rise or set; the earth turns. But they haven't changed their imagery or their language to reflect this knowledge; no one speaks of "morning earth turn" or "evening earth turn." Why is that? The evidence of the senses is so strong that it dictates the language we use; I can see the sun peeking above or sinking below the horizon, and it looks to me like the sun is rising or the sun is setting, so that's how I talk about it. It's faithful to the evidence of the senses. It's just not true.

So the evidence of the senses is mistaken about the sun. That's rather basic, and it's enough to make me question its accuracy on other matters. We disciples can understandably question just how much authority to give to sensory evidence by itself. Christians can legitimately claim that the revelation of Jesus Christ about human life and death is as convincing as the scientific investigations of Galileo about planetary motions. And that revelation is going to change the way we respond to those realities. We have more faith in the Word of God about resurrection than we do in the evidence of the senses about death, and that faith seems to be well placed, all things considered.

Do Christians go overboard in their belief in an afterlife? For one thing, I'm not sure Christians believe in an "afterlife." We certainly don't believe in one life lived here on earth for a certain number of years, ending in death, and then followed immediately by another, second life that is completely unconnected with that earlier life. However, Christians do believe in eternal life. We believe in one life, lived now with God in Christ by grace, and continued eternally in glory. The prayer of the church expresses it beautifully: "Lord, for your faithful people, life is changed, not ended."

Eternal life makes life on earth more important, not less. That's Jesus' whole point in his description of the Last Judgment in Matthew 25. If we have been just and merciful and loving with our needy brothers and sisters on earth for the love of God, then eternal life will be bliss. If we have not, it will be torture. This does not sound like a recipe for ignoring worldly matters in favor of fantasy; it sounds like a challenge to take this world very seriously indeed.

But then aren't we making God once again the hurler of damned souls into fire and brimstone? Not really. We are free to make our own choices about selflessness and selfishness. We are certainly urged to choose selflessness, but we are left free. Selfish people won't want to live forever in heaven. They won't fit in. The joy offered there is not their kind of joy.

The image I think of here is a family reunion. I think of family picnics in the park that I attended as a child and, later on, as a young man. It seems to me a most awkward and embarrassing idea to walk into the midst of the wrong family reunion by mistake. I wouldn't fit in. I wouldn't belong. I have nothing in common with them, and I can't go back in time and become a member now. It will be like that for the selfish and the unjust in eternity. They'd be misfits in heaven. In hell, they'll fit right in. It's a strong motive to avoid selfishness and injustice.

Pause & Pray

Matthew 25:31–40 Jesus describes the Last Judgment: a profile of the heaven-bound.

1 Thessalonians 4:13–18 Saint Paul describes our hope for resurrection in the risen Jesus.

1 John 3:1–3 Our eternal life is as certain as it is hidden from us now.

Do You Really Believe There's a Hell?

Does hell exist? The most comfortable and easy answer is no. A close second is the response of Abbé Arthur Mugnier, friend of Marcel Proust, and a gentle, kind French priest a century ago: "Yes, I believe in hell because it is a dogma of the church—but I don't believe anyone is in it."

Still, a person can freely say a final no to divine love. It takes a good deal of selfishness to say that no, but God must take the answer seriously and not force someone into heaven. God, who willingly loves us all, forces himself on no one.

But what is hell like? We don't know, but consider this image: Perhaps hell is not so very different from many a suburban living room; the crucial furnishings in each are a fireplace and a mirror.

In either heaven or hell we will gaze eternally on the one we adored in this life, so hell needs a mirror, for an eternity of self-absorption. For a time, self-absorption is an attractive activity in this life, if only for the self. It may look and feel good to us, whether we are famous or obscure.

Once, in a review of an autobiography, Dorothy Parker sarcastically said of the author: "The affair between Margot Asquith and Margot Asquith will live as one of the prettiest love stories in all literature."[4] Of course, one's selfishness and self-absorption are not pretty to others; they are boring almost immediately and, eventually, painful as well. Sometimes they are not attractive even to the self for an entire lifetime, and there's grace in that fact. Perhaps we will shift our gaze elsewhere, and be saved.

Children understand better than adults the potential hell of the living room. They catch on quickly to the irony of the room's name; many families do most of their daily living in every room except the living room. Ask any child to imagine a parent saying, "Go into the living room and stay there. You're never coming back. The rest of us will go on living in the other rooms. You'll stay in there alone, and no one will ever come in to bother you with a story or a game or dinner." The child's verdict: hell on earth.

But we aren't *sent* to the real hell; we *choose* it during this life. Often we choose it by degrees, wandering in and out and staying far too long. We are drawn by the self-centeredness, by the pretty furnishings, and by that mirror, into which we can gaze for hours and hours, or years and years. Meanwhile, who knows how many logs of others' lives are being consumed to keep that fire blazing just beneath the mirror of our self-regard?

In this image of hell, the fireplace is less interesting to me than the mirror, though more traditional. For centuries the artistic draftsmen of hell have agreed on the fiery torment, though some have considered freezing cold to be just as appropriate. Dante opted for both, in different precincts of the place. What's pertinent, though, is that the choices in life, the options for self or for God and others, go on and on forever.

All of which makes the mirror more fearsome for me. I imagine myself having briefly seen in judgment the face of a loving God, terminally alien to my lovelessness. After that experience, I imagine I'd prefer to cease to be—or, at least, I'd prefer to be in the dark—but certainly not to stare endlessly at my unloved and unloving face in the mirror, lit by the fire below.

Pause & Pray

Matthew 25:41–46 Christ describes the Last Judgment: a profile of those who are not heaven-bound.

Mark 14:17–21 "It would be better for that man if he had never been born."

Matthew 18:6–9 The eternal implication of sin.

Are Christians Taught to Despise the World?

A loveless selfishness can waste our life on earth and put eternal happiness at risk. Does that mean we should despise and fear this world we live in? Of course, the accusation that we Christians are urged to despise the world around us is related to that previous accusation concerning injustice. According to our critics, our problem as Christians is that we don't take this life seriously enough because we're so obsessed with the next one.

Unfortunately, some misguided Christians have given weight to such attacks because of their own insensitivity and lack of compassion or their substitution of an unhealthy otherworldliness for a genuinely Christian, incarnational worldview and spirituality. We disciples can be infuriating when we give the impression that our relationships with others, or with life in general, is just a practice session for the main event later on and really doesn't matter very much.

Such behavior reminds me of a story told by Fr. Alan Jones, dean of Grace Episcopal Cathedral in San Francisco. He described a dinner party he attended at which, during the time for cocktails and canapés, the hosts handed out little napkins with this inscription: "These are not hors d'oeuvres. This is dinner!" It was a practical joke, but it's a joke with a point. For Christians, life here and now is not hors d'oeuvres; it is dinner. Living and loving in the present are always the main course, and they determine much of the future, and all of eternity.

We disciples pray to go to heaven, and we claim that heaven is our ultimate goal. So what is heaven actually like? Saint Paul, drawing on the prophet Isaiah, tells us that we cannot know—or, more accurately, cannot take it in: "What eye has not seen, and ear has not heard, and what has not entered the human heart, what God has prepared for those who love him" (1 Corinthians 2:9). Of course, wisdom like that has seldom stopped a Christian writer from speculating, has it?

Isn't it odd that traditional Christian images of hell, though terrifying, seem so much more vivid and lively than the common images of heaven? Red devils wielding pitchforks among the leaping flames are much more riveting to the imagination than shapeless forms clad in white plucking stringed instruments while standing about on puffy clouds. It looks much safer and more comfortable than hell but so, well, dull. No wonder the Irish, a believing people but not a dull one, have a saying that we should choose heaven for the climate and hell for the company!

Indeed, generations of poets have romanticized Satan as a fascinating, almost heroic outcast and hell as his exile realm, where he is joined by all those too darkly proud to bend the knee. Those images make for lush poetry, but we need to remember the fireplace and the mirror. As a clincher, picture in your mind a month's vacation alone in a car with the most shallow, selfish, and self-centered person imaginable. Now change "month" to "eternal" and you're getting a truer picture of "the other place."

With regard to heaven, the human imagination fails, not the divine. Saint Paul writes to the Corinthians that we shall see God "face to face" (1 Corinthians 13:12) and know him even as he knows us. We shall see Love itself and Life itself! Heaven, as Romano Guardini expressed it, is where "God is alone with himself," and where we shall be united with him.[5]

But are there any human experiences that hint even feebly at what that means? Let me offer one. Think over your life and pick out one or two peak moments of love, especially love as reunion or forgiveness or reconciliation: a "starting over" with a loved one; a particularly moving experience of the sacrament of penance; a meeting with someone you love after a long separation. Think of the embrace, the elation, the ecstasy, and the undiluted, inexpressible joy. Now imagine that moment (for such experiences in this life are always momentary) as never-ending, as lasting forever. For as far as you can go with that image, it's a feeble hint at the unending aliveness and joy and fulfillment of heaven. It certainly beats learning the harp.

Pause & Pray

Mark 12:18–27 Jesus teaches what eternal life is like and what it is not like.

1 Corinthians 2:9 Saint Paul quotes Isaiah about our destiny as disciples.

chapter four

What Does
It Mean
to Be a
Disciple?

The news is good: A loving God has made us for his love. He saved us from our sins and called us to himself, now and forever. Still, the next question, for every generation of Christians, has been: Yes, but what difference does that make here and now? We likewise ask: What difference does it make for us that we are disciples? How does the Lord expect his followers to act? How do we choose his kingdom values rightly, and how do we sometimes go wrong?

Some have felt that being a disciple means that things ought to begin to pick up for us disciples right now, or very soon. Zebedee's wife may have been the first to approach it this way, in asking for special places for her sons in Jesus' throne room (Matthew 20:20–21). She certainly wasn't the last. It's an old answer, and an evergreen one, but it's wrong.

The difference the gospel of Jesus makes in the here and now is not that "things get better," but that we do. In their letters, both Peter and Paul make the connection between what God has become and done for us in Jesus Christ and what we disciples ourselves are now to become and do for God in his Son. Toward the end of his second letter, Peter writes of the second coming of Jesus, saying "what sort of persons ought [you] to be, conducting yourselves in holiness and devotion" (2 Peter 3:11). What does God call us disciples to do and become, for him and for one another, in response to the good news of the kingdom?

From the beginning, Christians have been idealists. Jesus constantly calls us to strive toward the ideal of being perfected "as your heavenly Father is perfect" (Matthew 5:48). We are to strive toward ideals that we most likely will never achieve, but the striving is what matters. We are to strive joyously, confidently, perseveringly, trusting in grace and not in a neurotic perfectionism that gives way to discouragement or bitterness. The silver may never be without its tarnish, but the polishing makes it shine.

Such idealism does not come easily. It goes against the grain of our culture. In the present age we value realism, not idealism. Take this simple test: When was the last time you said to someone, or someone said to you, "Oh, come on, be realistic!" Not long ago, probably. When was the last time you said to someone, or someone said to you, "Oh, come on, be idealistic!" Was it some while ago? But that is precisely what the gospel says to the Christian, over and over again, about everything: "Oh, come on, be idealistic!"

Pause & Pray

Matthew 5:21–22, 27–28, 31–48 In the Sermon on the Mount, Jesus calls his followers to be idealists.

Called to Conversion

It's usually easier for a disciple of Jesus at the beginning. Call it "first fervor" or the "honeymoon period" after conversion to living the Christian life. During those early days the enthusiasm and the sacrifices come more readily. However, we disciples are called to conversion all our lives long. Over and over again, we need to let Jesus change our minds and hearts about ourselves, about him, and about others. And our minds and hearts are the hardest things about us to change.

That's why Saint Paul is not quite my favorite hero or model of conversion. Ananias has that distinction. There are two men named Ananias in the Acts of the Apostles, and I do not mean the one who falls down dead after cheating the early Christian community in a shady real estate deal. For me, the patron saint of ongoing conversion is Ananias of Damascus; his dialogue with the Lord is an ideal example of daily conversion. Just listen in on a very important prayer experience in Ananias's life (important too for the future of the Christian church):

The Lord: Ananias.

Ananias: Here I am, Lord.

The Lord: Get up and go to the street called Straight and ask at the house of Judas for a man from Tarsus named Saul. He is there praying. . . .

Ananias: Lord, I have heard from many sources about this man, what evil things he has done. . . . And here he has authority from the chief priests to imprison all who call upon your name.

The Lord: Go, for this man is a chosen instrument of mine . . . (Acts 9:10–16).

Ananias is already a convert, a believer, a good person, active in ministry. As such, he has his sources of information and his firm opinions, and he can tell the Lord a thing or two about his people, and especially about his taste in leaders. Does any of this sound familiar? Still, Ananias is our patron saint of ongoing conversion and not a joke; he listens to the Lord, lets him change his mind and heart, and then goes off, humble, faithful, and trembling, toward the dangerous and the unknown.

When Ananias meets Paul, we find a powerful contrast: the blind man who can see, and the seeing man who is blind to a new spiritual reality. Ananias still does not "see" Saul as a convert and believer, while Saul, temporarily blinded, "sees" the meaning of Jesus in his life for the first time. Ananias imposes hands on Saul, and immediately the scales fall from Saul's eyes and his physical sight is restored. Saul has experienced initial conversion, and Ananias has experienced ongoing conversion.

Ananias has immediately begun to change his heart because of what the Lord Jesus told him. After his walk down Straight Street, Ananias greets the former enemy of the church by saying, "Brother Saul." That's a Christian disciple's faith, hope, and love in action.

Like Ananias, we disciples are constantly called to the changes of conversion, of seeing things differently. What we see differently may be our values, our priorities, our choices, our own worth or other people's, or our relationships. Think of a visit to an eye doctor. You sit in the darkened room, looking through lens after lens and hearing the question, "Now is this better or is *this* better?" (After a while, I can't tell one from another!) The exercise may be lengthy and difficult, but in the end you see better.

The Holy Spirit is the soul's eye doctor. If we give way to the grace of prayer, reflection, and discernment, we will begin to see better the way of the Lord for us in the midst of all the possibilities we could choose. Jesus becomes the light of our world, and as our seeing changes, we change our minds and hearts about lots of things, many times. Then, like Ananias, we can take a chance and do things for the Lord we never before would have believed that we could do—or that even needed doing.

But showing up is difficult, and so is keeping up the effort. It is so easy to promise ourselves that we will go see the eye doctor as soon as school is out or right after the holidays. Then years pass, and we get used to a dimmer view of things. Our eyes tire out easily. In our spiritual lives, we can show up less and less often for prayer; we can turn to the Lord less and less frequently as we get busier and busier with "life." No wonder Jesus asked the first disciples on one occasion, "But when the Son of Man comes, will he find faith on earth?" (Luke 18:8).

Much of the difficulty has to do with humility. Can we take the Lord's love and respect for us seriously enough that we love and respect ourselves as he does, in the face of our sins and imperfections? One temptation is to give up on ourselves; and this is the result of pride. We don't care whether or not God loves and accepts us, because we can't. It might be called "Marxist spirituality," named after Groucho, not Karl. The former once said that he wouldn't want to belong to a club that would accept him as a member. We may not want to belong to a God who could love and respect us, warts and all. Or we may be unwilling to let his evaluation replace our own, or even modify it.

Pause & Pray

Acts of the Apostles 9:10–20 The continuing conversion of Ananias of Damascus.

The F.O.E.

Another temptation is to make a separate peace with our main faults, to rationalize our choice to abandon the struggle against them. Sometimes this takes the form of what I call the "F.O.E.,"—the "Fallacy of the Opposite Extreme." The F.O.E. leads me to rationalize like this: I cannot take some fault of mine seriously, because then I would be in danger of going too far in the other direction. For instance, a friend urges me to work on my anger. What does he want me to do—become a human doormat? Or another friend suggests that I become a bit less miserly, a bit more generous. What does she want me to do, end up in the poorhouse? It's clearly a rationalization, but it works all too well in limiting spiritual growth. I can stand right here, next to the cliff, and pay no attention to everyone urging me to take a few steps back. Don't they realize I might fall into that river on the other side of the field? Imaginary dangers are so useful when resisting real change. (Political debates often abound in F.O.E.s.) Standing still spiritually is the greatest danger of all, if continuing conversion is essential to salvation—and it is.

Disciples in need of continuing conversion find so many ways to deny or avoid dealing with this need. Besides the

F.O.E., we have another powerful weapon for spiritual denial and resistance in the delaying tactic of the continuing resolution. We promise ourselves and the Lord that we are going to straighten up our lives, get our spiritual act together "tomorrow" or at least "soon." We want to tidy up our messy souls and then invite Jesus over for a really good visit, long overdue. We're forgetting that Jesus is not our guest. Rather, Jesus lives here in our souls; he is the owner and operator. We are not going to clean up, get new furniture, paint, or even "pick up around the place" without him.

Our call is not to "get ourselves ready for God" but to "let go" to him. If we are making bad judgments and bad choices (and everybody does), then the right move is not to change all the judgments and choices so that they will impress Jesus favorably the next time we get together with him. They probably won't, because they probably won't be much better than the ones they replaced, especially if we made them by ourselves, as usual.

No, the right move is to stop, look, and listen. We need to stop going it on our own, with just other folks as our models and advisors. We need to look long and hard at Jesus in the gospels, and we need to listen to his teachings and those of his church to find out what he considers important and valuable. Let's ask him, "Jesus, what do you want me to be like? What do you want me to do? How do you want me to judge myself and others, and situations in life?" Let's mean it when we ask it, let's ask it often, and let's never stop asking it.

If we do talk to Jesus like that, and then listen, what we will hear will challenge us, because Jesus does have a set of values for us. After all, values are assumptions about life, about what matters most. Almost everyone has a set of such values, good or bad or mixed, and we usually live and choose according to them. The values Jesus gives his disciples are not familiar to us from the world around us.

In fact, they turn worldly values upside down. The chief statement of them is called the Beatitudes (Matthew 5:3–12 and Luke 6:20–26), from the Sermon on the Mount and the Sermon on the Plain:

"Blessed are the poor in spirit,
for theirs is the Kingdom of heaven.

Blessed are they who mourn,
for they will be comforted.

Blessed are the meek,
for they will inherit the land. . . .

Blessed are the merciful,
for they will be shown mercy."

And the other five are just as unusual and unsettling! In Luke's version, there are "woes" as well.

Middle-Class Beatitudes

Several years ago I began to think of the unquestioned assumptions about life with which I grew up, in a nice middle-class Catholic home in the middle part of the twentieth century. I thought of how I bought into those assumptions and the gospel simultaneously, hardly noticing that there were tensions between the two sets of values, particularly when I judged or guided myself or others by the non-gospel values. Here then, with apologies to Matthew and Luke, are what I call my "Middle-Class Beatitudes":

Blessed are those who own their own homes.

Blessed are those who have a car, a stereo, and a hair dryer.

Blessed are those who go to college.

Blessed are those who can write their own ticket, are self-employed, keep getting better jobs, promotions, and more money.

Blessed are those who live on clean, well-lighted, safe streets.

Blessed are those who know the right people, have reservations, make wise investments, and can afford nice vacations.

Blessed are the winners.

Blessed are those who are charming, clever, witty, and can handle people well.

Blessed are those who live in a place where the movies are first-run and change weekly (my Southern California inculturation).

Blessed are those who get waited on in a store and don't have to wait on others themselves.

Blessed are those who can demand and get respect for who they are and for what they say and do.

Blessed are those with a high standard of living and a strong national defense.

Blessed are the young, the strong, the healthy, and especially those who are sexually attractive to one another.

Blessed are hospital patients only if they have a private room, or, if necessary, a semiprivate room, but in no case a bed in a ward.

Woe to renters, the unemployed, drifters, oddballs, the sick, the old, the poor, and people who talk out loud to themselves on the bus—avoid them like the plague, because losing is catching!

Are all those desirable things evil? No. May we kingdom people ever allow any of them to become primary, central, or ultimate? Again, no. Comfort, convenience, pleasure, and safety are all desirable, but they are not values central to the Christian gospel. If we disciples are going to keep turning more toward the Lord and less toward the world around us as our center in life, then we need to hold our values and our choices up to the light of the Beatitudes and Jesus more frequently. That's the meaning and content of ongoing conversion.

Pause & Pray

Matthew 5:3–12 Jesus teaches the values of the kingdom in the Beatitudes, the opening words of his Sermon on the Mount.

Luke 6:20–26 Luke's version of beatitude values in Christ's Sermon on the Plain.

Without continuing conversion we will live shallow spiritual lives. We will go through the motions of religion, investing as little of ourselves as we can. Picture a swimming pool. The Christians for whom the Middle-Class Beatitudes are central, controlling values will wade forever at the three-foot end of the pool. Spiritually, they won't get too wet, they won't drown, they will always be able to touch bottom, and it will be easy for them to get back out. They can easily walk to safety at the side if someone else starts to make waves. But they never swim! And isn't that the point of a swimming pool? Aren't we supposed to plunge into Jesus Christ, to get "lost" in him so that we can be "found"?

That's the danger of "cultural Christianity." We mistake going through the motions of Christianity for meeting

Jesus Christ. The former may lead to the latter, but not necessarily. That's why it's so safe in the middle of each December to ask each other, "Are you all ready for Christmas yet?" It's less safe to ask, "Are you all ready for Christ yet?" In the life of a disciple, though, that's what December and the other eleven months are for—getting ready for Christ, whenever we meet him. Like the good Samaritan we are trying to recognize him more often, to pass him by less frequently.

Sometimes we pass Jesus by because we have forgotten who we are, not who he is. The change is in us, not in him. (I am reminded of the story about Oscar Wilde, who said to an old acquaintance whom he had initially failed to greet, "Oh, I didn't recognize you. I've changed so lately.") In other words, we have forgotten we are Christians. In better moments we claim to be his, but then we wander far from him, still wearing his "uniform."

While the results of this process are usually sad, they can occasionally be hilarious as well. I remember a news story on television one weekend. A priest told the story on himself. He said that he was never in the habit of honking if he came up behind a car with a bumper sticker that urged him to do so. One day, though, he came up to a stoplight, and the sticker on the bumper in front of him read: "Honk if you love Jesus!" So he honked. The woman driving that car immediately leaned out the window and shouted back angrily, "Can't you see the light's red, stupid?"

It was funny that time, but so often people rightfully expect a Christ-like response from disciples who have "'Christian' written all over them" and are sadly disappointed. We are called to authenticity in our Christian life. It's a lifelong call, and it doesn't have to do with perfectionism. It has to do with consistency and commitment, and those are gifts we pray for, not accomplishments we come up with on our own.

87

Pause & Pray

Matthew 7:21–23 Actions, not words, prove we are followers of Jesus Christ.

Luke 6:46–49 Disciples don't build on sand, because they act on what they hear from Christ.

On Being Good Pharisees

Another threat to continuing conversion is self-righteousness. It's obvious to us that we disciples must resist what the baptismal rite calls the "glamour of evil." What's not so obvious is how attractive the evil of self-righteousness can be. When Jesus meets this evil in the Pharisees, it seems to upset him more than any other human failing. Perhaps that is because self-righteousness is so damaging to the "central nervous system" of Christian faith, Christ-righteousness. Our spiritual center is Jesus, not ourselves. If we are the source, the measure, and the chief beneficiaries of our own goodness, then there is no room for Jesus Christ in our lives. Remember Flannery O'Connor's dictum: Whoever doesn't need a savior can't have one. And Jesus, when speaking of seeking out the lost sheep, says, "I tell you, in just the same way there will be more joy in heaven over one sinner who repents than over ninety-nine righteous people who have no need of repentance" (Luke 15:7).

One of the meanings of this parable is that for Jesus the ninety-nine do not exist; everyone is the hundredth sheep. No one can say truthfully, "I have no need to repent. I am sinless." Anyone who says that is claiming to be self-righteous, not Christ-righteous; self-shepherding, not led by the Good Shepherd. He or she qualifies as a self-deceived modern Pharisee.

So what is the difference between those, on the one hand, who try sincerely but imperfectly to live as Christian disciples and those, on the other hand, who don't care one way or the other or even actively choose sin? Fancifully, we might say of the former that they are trying to be "good Pharisees."

Are there any good Pharisees? The gospels mention two of them. Joseph of Arimathea and Nicodemus are good Pharisees, people seriously committed to living virtuous religious and spiritual lives according to the Mosaic Law but also humble enough to respond to Jesus Christ by listening with open minds and hearts that they are willing to change if need be. Many practicing Christians find themselves in a similar situation. They have inherited religious beliefs and practices that they realize are not ultimate but means toward an end. The end is openness and responsiveness to a continuing relationship with Jesus Christ: personally, in his word, in his church, and in the circumstances and relationships of daily life.

Of course, there are risks in being a good Pharisee, the risks of prideful, judgmental self-righteousness. So what makes a Pharisee good? It consists in turning the Pharisaism upside down and making it serve oneness with Christ rather than self-glorification. The prayer of the Pharisee in the temple provides a clear example of bad Pharisaism: "O God, I thank you that I am not like the rest of humanity—greedy, dishonest, adulterous—or even like this tax collector. I fast twice a week, and I pay tithes on my whole income" (Luke 18:11–12). This is the only prayer Jesus Christ ever makes fun of; in fact, these verses show Jesus in a rare moment of satire.

How does a good Pharisee turn this arrogance upside down? By praying like this: "I thank you, God, that I am like the rest of men and women—imperfect and loved by you, sinful yet forgiven by you, unable to save myself spiritually and so embraced by you and your saving

Spirit." We are not thankful for our sins, but we are grateful for our awareness of them and for the humility, compassion, and forgiveness that are available to us from the Lord because of that awareness. An ancient prayer declares sin to be a *felix culpa*, a "happy fault," because the bad news of sinfulness is infinitely outweighed by the good news of the Savior, who came to deliver us from sin and lead us into the life of the kingdom.

Good Pharisees know they are sinners. This keeps them from becoming phonies. Jesus loved sinners and distrusted phonies. The world around us often taunts us with our imperfection and sinfulness, as if our faults prove that our Christian faith and practice are nothing but an empty show. And our failings would prove that, if we reacted to them defensively rather than humbly.

When someone says, "You Christians claim to be religious, but there are lots of people who don't believe or don't go to church and they live better lives than you," we must answer truthfully, "Ah yes, but think how much worse we would be without faith! You are right about us; we need to reform. We must try to do better. Please pray for us." That's the response of the sinner, the good Pharisee. The phony offers excuses and comparisons: "I was tired. I had a headache. It's the sort of thing I never do, actually. Besides, I'm not as bad as a lot of other people I can think of." There's no humility or repentance in that response, and it can't lead to forgiveness and renewal.

Because of hope, the Christian disciple's humility doesn't end in disappointment, depression, or even cynicism and despair. Hope is the confidence we have in Christ the Lover, and hence in ourselves, the ones he loves. We feel assured that God writes straight with our crooked lines; we know we need to keep trying to straighten ourselves out, but we also know that, whatever our limitations, God has none. Earthen vessels though we are, the Holy Spirit keeps using us as vessels of gospel life and action.

Without hope, it is possible for the Christian to give up, to become cynical about the ideals of discipleship. Like Aesop's fox beneath the grapes, we can drop out of the spiritual struggle because "no one ever makes it anyway." We tell ourselves it can't be done, and from there it is but a step to saying that those who are still striving are deluded or phony or both. This claim entitles us to sit on the sidelines and criticize those still in the race.

A lyric by Stephen Sondheim captures the essence of this spiritual condition. In his musical *Company*, an upper-middle-class divorcée who has had too much to drink sings a song entitled "The Ladies Who Lunch," in which she proposes a toast to different types of suburban matrons, skewering each one as she sings of them. Referring to the last type, her own, she mocks herself for her cynical tendency to just sit and watch disapprovingly, making sarcastic remarks as she sips her cocktail. Each moment is "another chance to disapprove. . . another reason not to move."[6]

To "just watch" is as deadly as it is tempting in the Christian life, picking out all the faults in the lives of imperfect disciples but not getting involved and connected. Jesus said, "He who is not with me is against me." Christian cynics snag themselves on that dichotomy.

The Keys of the Kingdom

In our search for images of Christian discipleship, we have chosen several that emphasize our behavior toward God and toward our neighbor because we see the true following of Christ in the most generous response possible to his two great commandments of love. Now though, we need to emphasize even more forcefully the attitudes and behavior of disciples toward each other in the church and toward all people in the world around them. Disciples cannot live a "Jesus and me" spirituality if their Father expects them to live a family life together as his children and if their Redeemer is going to judge them on the basis of their response to all their brothers and sisters, especially the "least" (Matthew 25:4–45).

A helpful image in this regard is the key. Jesus bestowed the keys to the kingdom on Peter as chief of the apostles (Matthew 16:19). Peter's successor continues to shepherd the flock within the church, the beginning of the kingdom of God here on earth, until each disciple is called home to the fullness of the eternal kingdom. But what about the other keys?

"The other keys" doesn't suggest a rival structure for governing the church. Rather, the phrase means that there's much more to daily Christian life than major decisions and a worldwide structure. The distinction between the kinds of keys brings to mind the story about the husband who claimed that he made the decisions on all the major questions facing his family, while his wife decided lesser matters, such as where they would both work, where they would live, and where their children would go to school. When asked what exactly were the major family issues that he decided, he gave such examples as what should be done about nuclear disarmament and global warming.

Major questions are important, but the day-to-day local decisions are much more numerous and just as vital, especially if we can actually do something about them. That's why there are many other keys to daily kingdom life besides those entrusted to Peter and his successors.

In particular, God has given all of us the keys to each other's hearts. No one has the keys to his or her own heart, to all the secret chambers that need opening up to the love of God and his family. We cannot forgive our own sins and we cannot love God by ourselves; for both

92

experiences we need each other. That's the way God has wisely and lovingly arranged the matter.

Furthermore, as a disciple, I do not know ahead of time who has a key to my heart, nor do I know to which hearts I have keys. That is the beauty and the risk of our life of grace together on earth. God chooses to love us, to heal us, to forgive us, to encourage and reassure us, through one another. Just take the word "encourage": it means literally to "put heart into" another. That is a daily activity not confined to great surgeons at major medical centers. It is the call of each disciple.

In a culture devoted to self-realization, self-fulfillment, and independence, a plan of grace that demands such personal interdependence may seem like divine effrontery. But we have strayed wide of the mark, and God has not. He who is love did not love us and make us free so that we could be hermetically independent of him and one another. Rather, he loved us so much he made us free to love him and each other.

Individualism and fierce independence take us only so far, and rarely in the direction of loving, or being loved by, anyone except ourselves. The most basic experiences of human existence are made holy by grace, and they are impossible without others who love us enough to make them happen.

This is true throughout our lives: we did not generate ourselves in love; we did not nurse ourselves; we did not teach or evangelize ourselves; we did not create our own personal gifts and skills, nor did we discover or develop them alone; fortunately, we did not fall in love only, or even mainly, with ourselves; we sought pardon, but others had to give it; we needed caring and gentleness and strong challenges from others, and they were there for those times too. Our lives will continue this way to their end: we hope not to grow old alone; when we do get sick, we cannot visit ourselves in the hospital; we cannot hold our own hands when we die, or bury ourselves, or pray afterward for the repose of our own souls. Independence is no doubt a fine and healthy goal in its way, but the banquet of Christian life, here and in eternity, is decidedly not "a table for one."

"I'm Spiritual, but I'm Not Religious"

In the matter of religion and spirituality, our American obsession with individualism is often reinforced by disillusionment with the imperfections, sins, and hypocrisy found within organized religion. Young people especially experience strong yearning for spirituality, for a relationship with a power or reality transcending their experience of themselves, but they do not trust churches. These days we often hear people say, "I'm spiritual, but I'm not what you'd call religious."

As Christians, we need to meet such statements with understanding, not derision. Nevertheless, we also need to be honest about our belief that Jesus Christ founded the church and called his followers to live their lives within it. Father Andrew Greeley has reminded us that the church will not be perfect because its human members are imperfect and sinful.

We disciples of Jesus can't be spiritual without being religious. Consider, for instance, the matter of worship. We hear people say, "I don't go to church on Sunday. I don't believe in cooping myself up in a stuffy building on a beautiful morning. I feel much closer to God when I'm taking a hike through the beautiful hills and mountains he created."

That's their choice, but it's not who we disciples are. Christians are not a people who believe that Jesus, on the night before he died, gathered with his friends in the upper room, turned to them, and said, "Go take a hike in memory of me." Rather, we believe that Jesus, on the night before he died, took bread, blessed and broke it, and gave it to his apostles, saying, "Take this and eat, this is my body." Then Jesus took a cup and gave it to them, saying, "All of you must drink from it, for this is my blood." Then he said, "Do this as a remembrance of me."

So on Sunday, the Lord's day, the disciples of Jesus gather and celebrate Eucharist, doing this in memory of him. We believe it gives so much meaning to everything about our lives, including the hike we take through the beautiful hills on Sunday afternoon.

Pause & Pray

John 6:53–58 We are joined to Christ and his people, now and forever.

Luke 22:14–20 Jesus at the Last Supper: "Do this in memory of me."

The Bodies of Christ

We must be alert to the moments each day when we are privileged to act with the love of Christ in the lives of others, when we become aware that he has given us one of those keys to hearts in the kingdom. No matter how small the opportunity seems to us, it matters to the Lord. With his doctrine of the Mystical Body of Christ, Saint Paul boldly describes the essential importance of the loving service and care of disciples for one another. He teaches that the followers of Jesus are as necessary and as intimately joined to each other as the different organs of a single human body (1 Corinthians 12:12–27; Colossians 3:15; Ephesians 1:18–23).

The Mystical Body of Christ is a wondrous image, but one in constant danger of functioning at the level of a cliché, if it functions for some disciples at all. This inspired image can become empty and vague, half-heard and then ignored, not because it lacks force in itself but because we fail to put it into force in our daily lives. Hearing a "Body of Christ" passage from Saint Paul proclaimed in church can become like receiving a letter from our high school or college alumni association. We are familiar with this kind of letter: it begins with a sentence that runs: "No matter how far we roam, guys and gals, we'll always be Trojans at heart (or Bruins or Wildcats or whatever)!" Yeah, yeah. Sure, sure. But what does that have to do with anything beyond our checkbooks?

For contrast, let's look at our attitudes and behavior toward the sacramental Body of Christ, the Eucharist. The Eucharist is important and special for us. We would not knowingly receive it unworthily. We genuflect before the reserved sacrament in the tabernacle, we remain reverently quiet in church, and we periodically tone down the restless children. In fact, though, we are quite capable of genuflecting and making the Sign of the Cross reverently upon leaving church, only to tear into some member of the Mystical Body of Christ the moment we get in the car or even as soon as we hit the parking lot.

I am not setting up a dichotomy here; this is not an either-or matter. Rather, it is a question of both-and. Because of Eucharist we must cherish and reverence our brothers and sisters in Christ; they are the church with and in and for whom we offer Eucharist. And all peoples are included, as we lift the entire redeemed creation to the Father in Christ in the liturgy. So reverence for both dimensions of the Body of Christ is demanded of us. Often enough, reverence for the sacrament has much to teach us about reverence for the people.

And make no mistake: there is a priority here. The sacramental Body of Christ exists for the sake of the Mystical Body of Christ. The Eucharist is food for our journey here on earth, and the People of God remember Christ in liturgy until he comes again. In heaven there will be no 10:30 Sunday morning Mass, no Blessed Sacrament chapel, and no all-night adoration. However, there will always be our brothers and sisters in the Mystical Body of Christ. A word to the wise, then: if our genuflections and conduct in church are devout, but our words and actions toward others are careless, let's not shift the emphasis; let's just extend it from the sacrament to the people—soon, and permanently.

Pause & Pray

1 Corinthians 11:23–32 In this earliest description of Christian Eucharistic worship, Saint Paul relates the receiving of the Body and Blood of Christ to our worthy behavior as Christians.

Galatians 5:13–15 Freedom in Christ is freedom to love one another, not a license to cause harm.

Because the Eucharist is perfect but we are not, these words of wisdom are hard to put into practice. Many a committed and hard-working disciple wrestles with the problem of harshness in speech. Ministers, ordained and unordained, find it difficult to be gentle, toward themselves as well as toward others. An edge of judgment and self-righteousness creeps so easily into our remarks to and about each other. Impatience and gossip are ants at the picnic of Christian living.

Why is this so? I have two hunches, one about human nature and the other about the difficulty of living the Christian virtues. Oscar Wilde is our expert for the first hunch. In the second act of his classic comedy, *The Importance of Being Earnest,* two young women mistakenly believe that they are in love with the same man, and they begin to fight over him by insulting each other. Building up to an insult, one of the two characters says: "On an occasion of this kind it becomes more than a moral duty to speak one's mind. It becomes a pleasure."[7]

How deftly Wilde skewers the human urge to use truth as the cloak behind which to hide the dagger of intent—to get in a brutal jab! It is a sinful human tendency to use the truth as a club on one another, but God's grace cannot heal us until we open our self-righteous, self-justifying indignation to that grace. Often enough we are in pain ourselves, and we want to strike back. That's understandable, but it only leads to more conflict, and it flies in the face of the call of Jesus to turn the other cheek. Impractical and idealistic as that call may sound to us, Jesus issued it, knowing that only in that way would peace come about. Anger eludes healing as long as it parades as virtuous indignation.

Which brings us to the other hunch, and to Fr. J. B. Scaramelli, an eighteenth-century priest writing on discernment of spirits, who drew up two lists: one of genuine virtues of the Christian life, and the other of their counterfeits, vices that masquerade as virtues. Of interest to us here is the vice he listed as the phony version of charity—"bitter zeal."[8]

What a shrewd insight! How many of the tapes in our heads and the diatribes in our conversation start out with bitter zeal. It might sound something like this: "Well, I'm sorry to have to say this, but it seems nobody but me gives a damn what becomes of this parish (or program, or school, or hospital, or meeting, or whatever)!" By then, we have moved completely, if gradually, from doing God's will in a situation to imposing our own or venting our spleen. When our concern is gentle, forgiving, compassionate, and meek, it is much more likely to do the work of Christian love than when it scorches all the earth—and earthlings—in its path.

Pause & Pray

James 1:26–27 There is no genuine Christian spirituality without disciplined speech.

James 3:1–12 The disciple of Jesus is challenged to charitable speech. "The tongue is a small member and yet has great pretensions."

"I Knew All I Had to Do Was Call Your Attention to It."

But attack is not the greatest danger in Christian interaction. More often, disciples run the risks of ignoring or taking for granted their sisters and brothers in Christ. There's a scene in Thornton Wilder's play *Our Town* that helps me to picture what God must make out of our treatment of each other. It is evening in a small New England town in the first quarter of the twentieth century, and a father is alone with his teenage son, to whom he says very quietly:

> Well, George, while I was in my office today I heard a funny sound . . . and what do you think it was? It was your mother chopping wood. There you see your mother—getting up early; cooking meals all day long; washing and ironing—and still she has to go out in the back yard and chop wood. I suppose she just got tired of asking you. She just gave up and decided it was easier to do it herself. And you eat her meals, and put on the clothes she keeps nice for you, and you run off and play baseball—like she's some kind of hired girl we keep around the house but don't like very much. [Pause] I knew all I had to do was call your attention to it. Here's a handkerchief, son.[9]

99

This scene brings to mind so many relationships in which we run the risk of taking someone for granted. It may not even be someone who does something for us, like George's mother in the play. It may be someone for whom we need to do something. Jesus Christ has told his disciples that he will come to them in their family, friends, neighbors, and strangers, especially those who are most needy: "For I was hungry and you gave me food, I was thirsty and you gave me drink, a stranger and you welcomed me, naked and you clothed me, ill and you cared for me, in prison and you visited me" (Matthew 25:35–36).

Jesus our King leaves us in each other's charge in the kingdom on earth, and he tells us, "You are loved, trusted, entrusted with one another, counted upon, in charge, responsible for yourselves and others, for the kingdom, the church, the world." And then he comes to us in the talkative people and the uncommunicative ones, in the boring, the gossipy, the angry, the lonely, the depressed, the homeless, the unreasonable. And it is our task to open to them our minds, our attention, our hearts, our loving wills, our purses, our wallets, and our energies.

Certainly it is not our vocation as disciples to become "doormats for Jesus," trodden flat in service, because our stewardship extends to ourselves as well. We concluded that when we looked at Jesus saying no. But there is a balancing truth here: our vocation in life is not to become "bulldozers for ourselves." We are properly stewards over our own gifts and welfare, but this stewardship is best exercised by a modest "department of consumer affairs" within each of us, not by turning our entire life into a consuming affair.

With Thornton Wilder's father and son in mind, we disciples can easily imagine God our Father, saying to each of us, "I listened recently and heard something I didn't like to hear. I've seen and heard it before many times. I saw your sisters and brothers in need of you. Some of my son's people went without what they needed because of you. It's your job. Jesus had to find other means for them, or no means at all. Jesus feeds you with his body, teaches you his word, gives you his life, provides for your needs, listens to your prayers, forgives your sins. He's your servant and your brother, but he's also your Redeemer and your Master." And then, because God doesn't want our guilty feelings but our love in action instead, he adds, ever so gently, "I knew all I had to do was call your attention to it."

Pause & Pray

1 Corinthians 13:1–7 The supreme ideal of the Christian disciple is love.

chapter five

Why and How
Does a
Disciple Pray?

*L*et's suppose we disciples are taking the Christian life seriously: How do we listen and talk to God without trying to control him or without giving up and running away?

There are many guides available to us for our personal prayer, classic writers such as Saint Teresa of Avila and Saint John of the Cross, as well as modern companions such as Thomas Merton, Anthony Bloom, and Thomas Green, among so many others. But we need more than guides. We need to see ourselves as persons of prayer. Even that phrase, "person of prayer," can intimidate many a follower of Jesus Christ. The image of a saint levitating in wordless contemplation—or, at least, of someone who can keep his or her mind on God and off the bank balance for two minutes in succession—can put us off prayer. As a consequence, we sometimes do not approach prayer with confidence in God who dwells within us, and perhaps, after some discouraging experiences, we just don't approach prayer at all.

Although we need personal prayer, we do not need prayer that seems like homework handed in to God, or like performing for Jesus on the high wire of thought, or like a debt to be paid off daily. We need prayer that is time spent—"wasted," if you will—listening to God's word and responding. We need to listen and respond with both mind and heart, because that's what friends do together. We cannot become and remain intimate friends of Jesus Christ if we are never alone with him, opening our hearts to him as he opens his to us.

A Tale of Two Benches

That kind of time with the Lord is often a "hard sell" for disciples today. My own suspicion is that our struggle to pray can be called "A Tale of Two Benches." The two benches are the park bench and the bus bench. I go to the bus bench pragmatically, to wait for transportation, and a successful visit is as brief as possible. While there, I may restlessly crane my neck to see if that truck in the distance is really my bus. I may bring something to read, so I won't waste any time. I may remark to others waiting there that bus service certainly isn't what it used to be.

But I go to the park bench for its own sake. I may sit in silence, with birds singing, children playing, and the sun shining through the leaves of the trees. Nothing is produced. Nothing gets done.

My guess is that 90 percent of what we do during our conscious moments on any given day is useful, productive "bus-bench" activity. Prayer, however, is the quintessential "park bench" activity, and when we inveterate bus benchers come to it, we can too easily arrive with our bus bench expectations in command, with frustration a likely result. Over and over again, we need to make the difficult but essential choice to let go of those expectations and permit the Lord to lead us to the park.

This image helps to explain our common complaint that "nothing happens" when we try to pray. If indeed "everything is grace," then something wondrously important has already happened every time a disciple even tries to pray: God has come in search of his daughter or son, not the other way around. He has given the grace, the call to prayer.

Pause & Pray

Hosea 1:16 The prophet compares God's dealing with Israel (and each soul) to his own dealing with his estranged wife.

Matthew 6:6 The values of solitude and humility in Christian prayer.

Revelation 3:20 The links between prayer, Eucharist, and the promise of eternal life.

Tiny Time Pills

If prayer is turning our minds and hearts to God, then it is likely that the most significant effects of prayer will take place in those minds and hearts. The most important effect of prayer is not necessarily how we feel during prayer or immediately afterward. Prayer is not a "fix," it is listening with faith, hope, and love.

Some years ago a new cold remedy came on the market that claimed an effectiveness that lasted for many hours because of all the "tiny time pills " in each capsule which would keep on working long after the medicine had been taken. The miniature pills were coated with different thicknesses and therefore took different lengths of time to dissolve, enter the bloodstream, and go to work against the cold.

So what? Well, many of us who try to pray assume that, if "it's working," we will "feel something" during the prayer time and immediately afterward. Sometimes we do feel something, but probably our assumption is wrong. When we talk and listen to each other, we often have to go away to think about and feel through the conversation, to size it up against life experiences, to sleep on it, and then get back together and respond anew. Can't we assume that the way God listens and speaks to us is at least as subtle and continuous as our listening and speaking to each other? His word to me this morning can be somewhat like that capsule of medicine, its various components "going off" in my life this afternoon, tomorrow, next week, or next year.

Often when a disciple has been praying for a while, the initial positive feelings, or "consolations," taper off and cease. God moves the disciple along to a different way of experiencing him, often with a certain dryness. Fr. Thomas Green, S.J., has written superbly of this experience in *When the Well Runs Dry,* a greatly reassuring guide for the journey of prayer:

> Our experience of dryness in prayer, then, is not merely a frustrating experience of the absence of God. It is an essential experience of our identification with Jesus, who "learned obedience through suffering." More concretely still, the Lord allows it so that we may "learn obedience through suffering," that we may

acquire that passion for God of which Kierkegaard speaks, that passion for the Father's will that possesses Jesus in St. John's Gospel.[10]

Guidance in prayer can be important for us disciples. Whether it is spiritual reading, spiritual direction, or both, help is available, and often crucial, for the disciple trying to pray. As persons of prayer, we are tempted to compare ourselves to others and to imagine ourselves as inferior and not "cut out for it." We are wrong on both counts. Other disciples may well not be as lofty as we imagine them to be, and even if they are, so what? Each person's prayer is as individual and unique to him or her as a letter written to a parent or a friend.

Imagine feeling so self-conscious about our relationship with a close friend that we cannot make a phone call to that person without evaluating how it's going at each moment and then giving ourselves a grade on the entire exchange after it's over. If we kept on analyzing and anguishing like that, we'd end up dialing the number less and less often. Perhaps as infrequently as we come to prayer.

"Open wide and say 'Ah!'" That's good advice at the doctor's office, and it's not bad advice about prayer as well. So much of our "bus bench" activity is filled with competition, calculation, and evaluation that we need to shift gears when we come to prayer. We need to experience the rich passivity of opening ourselves to God—our eyes and ears as well as our hearts and minds—to God's loving word in creation, in Scripture, and in life around us. We don't open wide enough often enough to divine presence and love, so we end up saying "Ah!" far too rarely. It seems difficult to do after a while, so we keep choosing what we feel good at and familiar with instead.

In that sense prayer is a struggle, and, in the present spiritual environment, it is even a countercultural activity. Many years ago the British playwright Enid Bagnold, author of *The Chalk Garden,* vividly described this experience of resistance to prayer:

> How boldly we waste our time—when we know there is so little of it. How we know nothing—and would rather garden than think of it. How the slightest diversion makes one fling off the tedium of contemplating God. Life is wasted, flung away hourly in expectation. The days run by, decoyed by it. Even in getting up we expect breakfast. Then there is Monday . . . and Saturday . . . and Christmas. . . . Or—if we are left in a pool of silence—let's cut our nails.[11]

Followers of Jesus can start out as disciples, for whom Christian life and service is a labor of love—but without the regular, loving spiritual intimacy of prayer, the disciple may dwindle into a mere "church person," for whom the whole experience has itself dwindled into a love of labor. After that, given enough time and problems, faith can shrivel and die. Yet Jesus wants to teach us to pray as lovingly as he taught those first disciples on the hillside. It is for us to turn to him again and again and let him do so.

A Modern Addiction and the Challenge to Pray

More and more I am convinced that the complaint "I don't have time to pray" is a dodge. Many of us say something like that so we won't have to face the real problem. Certainly, everyone is busy, but we all find time for twenty-one meals a week and for all the snacks in between. In fact, the busier Americans get, the fatter they become. We never hear it said of someone, "He died of malnutrition. He just couldn't find time to eat."

There is an addiction, widespread in our national culture, that directly threatens a Christian life of prayer. The addiction is stress. Consider Dr. Gerald May's masterful description of the impact of stress addiction on prayer from his classic *Addiction and Grace*:

> In most average cases of stress addiction, people simply find they need extra time to wind down before they can begin to relax. Some individuals know this pattern so well that they plan their vacations around it. "I have to take at least a two-week vacation because it takes me almost a week to relax, then a few days just to sleep, and then I can have a couple of really enjoyable days." With more severe stress addiction, people may be totally unable to relax unless they do something that gives them their fix of stress chemicals. Many people choose jogging or some other physically stressing activity. Such activities have become immensely popular among the stress-addicted because they provide enough chemicals to keep withdrawal symptoms at bay, while at the same time freeing the mind from normal worries and work tasks.
>
> It is in the realm of spiritual practice, however, that attachment to stress becomes most obvious. Spending time in quiet, receptive openness is an essential part of prayer, meditation, and most other spiritual practices. In such settings, even mild addiction to stress becomes rapidly and painfully evident. For many modern spiritual pilgrims, the simple matter of taking time for daily prayer can become a battle of will excruciatingly reminiscent of that encountered in chemical addiction. The mind can generate wondrous excuses to do something instead of just being open and present. The struggles that go on between being and doing can be awesome.

Issues of control and will power, surrender and defeat rage with all the drama of true spiritual warfare.

There are many things all of us might rather avoid in prayer: we might rather not relinquish our sense of self-mastery; we might rather not hear what God might ask of us; we might rather avoid the self-knowledge that comes to us in quiet. Now, in addition, increasing numbers of us are discovering that we would rather not experience the discomfort of being peaceful.[12]

Some of us disciples need to do more than pencil prayer in the appointment book again and again. We may need to consider the larger question of stress addiction and address it in a broad way that includes our response to the call to prayer.

Cyranos at Prayer?

Edmond Rostand, a French playwright of a century ago, provides our final image of the disciple considering prayer. His most enduring play, *Cyrano de Bergerac*, features a hero who is a great-hearted soldier and poet afflicted with a nose so large that he is certain he could never win the love of his beloved Roxane.[13] So Cyrano stays behind the scenes, writing beautiful love letters for the handsome but tongue-tied young soldier with whom Roxane has fallen in love. Only at the end of Cyrano's life does Roxane discover that the heart's expressions with which she fell in love belonged not to the handsome soldier but to Cyrano. It is a grandly romantic work, and it's never off the stage or screen for long.

Think of God as the beautiful beloved. Sometimes disciples can stay away from him, in the spiritual shadows, because they imagine that their sins and limitations prevent their stepping forward and declaring their love boldly and openly. To vary the plot a bit, perhaps they feel tongue-tied as well as ugly. They are certain that the terrible impression they make on God will smudge or even wipe out the yearning love they feel and want to express. The most discouraged may slip away altogether, while others just work and serve harder behind the scenes, hoping that greater "usefulness" will fill in for the intimacy with God that seems impossible.

The play about Cyrano is sad enough, but not as sad as disciples who won't trust God to love them and listen to them as much as they long for him to do—no matter how ugly or tongue-tied they feel. When I was a young man and first saw José Ferrer play Cyrano on screen, I wanted to shout at him "Oh, tell her it's you! Tell her you love her!" But maybe Cyrano was right. Perhaps Roxane wouldn't have been smart enough and good enough to recognize her man when she saw him. But there's no such danger with God.

Oh, tell him it's you! Tell him you love him! And tell him everything that's in your heart, good or bad. Can't you see he loves you?

Pause & Pray

2 Corinthians 12:7–10 Saint Paul learned in prayer: The Lord Jesus doesn't love us because we are strong; his love makes our weakness strong in him.

chapter six

How Are Disciples Called to Serve in Ministry?

ow are disciples called to minister to each other and the world, side by side, in servant fashion? How do we serve God in the church without becoming proud, judgmental, or selfish loners?

The style and even the content of Christian ministries have undergone challenging transformations since the Second Vatican Council. We disciples need to imagine ourselves and the church in the light of our call to follow in the steps of Jesus. We do this most profoundly when we pray and reflect upon our shared mission of building up and serving the church in the world. This is a need not so much for techniques and programs as for vision, motivation, and perseverance.

The Council fathers themselves described best how we are in this ecclesial, ministerial vocation together:

> For this the Church was founded: that by spreading the kingdom of Christ everywhere for the glory of God the Father, she might bring all men to share in Christ's saving redemption. . . . All activity of the Mystical Body directed to the attainment of this goal is called the apostolate, and the Church carries it on in various ways through all her members. For by its very nature the Christian vocation is also a vocation to the apostolate. . . . [T]he member who fails to make his proper contribution to the development of the Church must be said to be useful neither to the Church nor to himself.[14]

This strong statement pictures a church in which each member receives gifts from God that he or she puts at the service of the life of the church in its mission to proclaim and extend the kingdom in the world. It does not portray a church in which an elite leadership is herding a large and silent flock through this life unto eternity. Nor does it imagine a church in which all members are on their own, "freelancers for Jesus," striking out in whatever directions appeal to them for as long as those paths seem attractive or fashionable.

All Christian leadership, then, demands "followership," that is, discipleship: a following of Jesus Christ, who is not safely dead, risen, ascended, remote, and out of the way of our wills, our plans, and our opinions. Instead, as disciples we follow Jesus Christ who is alive, well, and active in the church. It is a church full of our willing, planning, and opinionated sisters and brothers, to whom he also speaks, leads, and through whom he sometimes follows us. The American bishops' document on the Sunday homily, "Fulfilled in Your Hearing," makes the point that the church needs offices and ministries but that they are secondary, because the primary reality is the presence of Christ in the assembly.[15]

God wills the salvation of all peoples, and he wills that all disciples collaborate with him and with one another in this saving work. The task of harmonizing all the gifts of Christians in the continuing action of the Savior is the task of the church's entire lifetime, and of the lifetimes of all disciples.

Pause & Pray

Ephesians 4:1–16 The Holy Spirit unites disciples and their different gifts into the one Body of Christ, drawing them to be one in loving service.

"You Give Them Something to Eat"

In the face of numberless and overwhelming needs, discouraged disciples are sometimes tempted to turn away entirely. Recall how ready the first disciples were to send the hungry thousands away to find food for themselves. Jesus, whom these thousands had followed, challenged his disciples: "Give them some food." They responded that the little they had could make no difference. Jesus' answer has this sense to it: "Give what you have to me, and we'll see." All were fed, with much left over (Mark 6:34–44).

I think of this image of Jesus when I drive down a city street these days. I come to a stop at an intersection and see a homeless person at the curbside holding up a sign that says Will Work For Food. My feelings are mixed: I don't have a job to offer the person; I don't know whether a donation would really go for food; I don't know whether the little I could come up with would help much; I don't even know whether the light is just about to change! On the other hand, I have a deep sense that I would prefer to meet Jesus in judgment as a sucker who got taken by a few of the several people I helped rather than as a shrewd fellow who never got taken because he never gave.

These are difficult questions without easy answers. But there is no denying how fundamental those words are: Will Work For Food. We dare not scorn someone who carries such a sign, because those words are also ours. And they were Christ's words before he made them ours: "My food is to do the will of the one who sent me and to finish his work" (John 4:34). Doing the Father's will nourished Jesus with the Father's love and his own response to that love. Will Work For Food.

Now those four words belong to us disciples. We approach the altar, celebrate Eucharist with one another, and receive the body and blood of Christ, the bread from heaven, to nourish and strengthen us for our journey. The purpose of this journey is the deepening of kingdom life within ourselves, the living of it with one another, and the proclamation of it to the world, leading all to eternal life: Will Work For Food.

This purpose sounds loftier and nobler than we often feel. We can become discouraged, bored, tired, selfish, envious, or some combination thereof. We feel like working our own wills, not God's; following our own paths, not Jesus Christ's. The Lord told a very helpful parable that addresses those very feelings:

> "What is your opinion? A man had two sons. He came to the first and said, 'Son, go out and work in the vineyard today.' He said in reply, 'I will not,' but afterwards he changed his mind and went. The man came to the other son and gave the same order. He said in reply, 'Yes, sir,' but did not go. Which of the two did his father's will?" They answered, "The first." Jesus said to them,

> "Amen, I say to you, tax collectors and prostitutes are entering the kingdom of God before you."
>
> —MATTHEW 21:28–31

Even though Jesus originally directed this story at the chief priests and elders, we can easily find applications to ourselves. The insincerity of the second son is obvious, but the struggle of the first son may have even more to say to disciples. The young man didn't want to do what his father asked. We often prefer to do what we feel like doing, what we're good at, what we've been doing for a while (and the same way we've been doing it), even if it's no longer what the king wishes or what the kingdom needs from us.

We are usually willing to do "A+" work for Jesus, work that chimes right in with our gifts. We are less ready to do "C+" work for the Lord: work we're not particularly good at, that we find much harder, less rewarding and affirming, but work that needs to be done by us right now, because we are the ones on the scene who are called to do it.

Pause & Pray

Matthew 21:28–31 Each of the two sons in the parable is imperfect, but one is far better, because, in the kingdom, actions trump words.

That "C+" work for the kingdom could be anything calling for patience, forgiveness, compassion, understanding, and self-sacrifice. It calls us out of ourselves to others, and to the Other. It can be work that will remain unglamorous and unfinished, like the care of the poor and the needy. We are tempted to say, with those disciples clutching their loaves and fish, "What can one person do in the face of all this?" The answer from the Lord is, "Whatever you as one person can do—do it! Do it with the faith that you are working in me and I am working in you. And if all my sisters and brothers work, I will bless it, break it, and it will be enough."

There can be no room for "Christian fatalism" in the face of problems around us. We live in a society that has swerved from its course lately and driven very fast down a sinister detour of selfishness and self-absorption. As the social scene darkens, the vehicle slows down and some people start to look for familiar landmarks, addresses, or at least a correct turn. We disciples of Jesus need to take to heart and live out the truth of the prophetic insight of Thomas Merton in his introduction to *The Prison Meditations of Father Alfred Delp* (a priest killed by the Nazis in early 1945): "The supposed 'creativity' claimed by the untrammeled subjectivism of men who seek complete autonomy defeats itself, because man centered on himself inevitably becomes destructive."[16]

The humanism of Father Delp, which is also the humanism of the church, recognizes that man has to be rescued precisely from this spurious autonomy that can only ruin him. He must be liberated from fixation on his own subjective needs and compulsions and recognize that he cannot fully become himself until he knows his need for the world and his duty of serving it.

If selfishness is not to be the dynamic of our lives, what is this "fulfilling selflessness" supposed to do? Again we listen to Merton, drawing from Father Delp's meditations:

> In bare outline, man's service of the world consists not in brandishing weapons to destroy other men and hostile societies, but in creating an order based on God's plan for his creation, beginning with minimum standards for a truly human existence for all men. Living space, law

and order, nourishment for all, are basic needs without which there can be no peace and no stability on earth. "No faith, no education, no government, no science, no act, no wisdom will help mankind if the unfailing certainty of the minimum is lacking."[17]

We need to choose our values, set our priorities, and make our daily choices more and more as disciples of Jesus Christ and less and less as consumers centered on ourselves. As daughters and sons of the Father, we may feel reluctant and we may occasionally show up late, but we need to get up and go out to the particular vineyard in which the Lord is calling us to join him in his work of mercy and love.

A Magnificent Invalid

The theater of Western Europe has been called "a magnificent invalid": after twenty-five hundred years of "the worst season ever," it is still going strong. Because humanity refuses to do without drama and theater, all the flops, failures, and dreadful excesses cannot kill our love of the live performance. Some critic can always sell an article to a magazine about the imminent death of theater; fifty years later the writer and the journal are gone, but the curtains are still going up.

In the realm of grace, something similar might be said about the church. All the sins, betrayals, persecutions, rigidity, and mediocrity in human responses to the divine call cannot put out the flame of the Holy Spirit. Nevertheless, the human "church of the headlines" can seem like an invalid indeed. During this recent terrible scandal of child sexual abuse by some priests, and failure to deal with it by some bishops, great harm was done to victims and much damage was done to the church. Through justice, healing, and reconciliation all concerned can move from shame to hope.

119

Still, neither horrible sins nor newspaper headlines can sum up a church or a people. The German people are not merely their Nazi past. Americans aren't summed up by the story of slavery. Headlines never tell the entire story of a people, because headlines record the exceptional, not the usual. Only planes that crash make headlines. If all we knew of air travel were drawn from the front page of the newspaper, we would never board another flight.

Certainly, there are problems and crises within the church, and there always have been. They are evident to any honest eye, and they give proof of the earthen character of our role as vessels. But the magnificence of the church is in her people, and in their faith and works, seen family by family, street by street, parish by parish, around the diocese and around the world.

That's the wondrous paradox of being a magnificent invalid—in the church's case, the most magnificent of all. This sense of the paradoxical in the life of the church and the disciple was powerfully described by Saint Paul:

> In everything we commend ourselves as ministers of God, through much endurance, in afflictions, hardships, constraints, beatings, imprisonments, riots, labors, vigils, fasts; by purity, knowledge, patience, kindness, in a holy spirit, in unfeigned love, in truthful speech, in the power of God; with weapons of righteousness at the right and at the left; through glory and dishonor, insult and praise. We are treated as deceivers and yet are truthful; as unrecognized and yet acknowledged; as dying and behold we live; as chastised and yet not put to death; as sorrowful yet always rejoicing; as poor yet enriching many; as having and yet possessing all things.
>
> —2 Corinthians 6:4–10

Paul did not view the church through rose-colored glasses or the refraction of despondency but with the eyes of faith. It is a less melodramatic and more complicated view than we sometimes read or hear about, but its challenge and its reassurance are clear.

The image of the magnificent invalid has its value at the level of the individual disciple as well. Owning up to our own limitations and powerlessness permits the Lord's gracious action to activate our gifts much more effectively than we are able to do on our own. The encounter between Peter and the crippled beggar in the Temple after Pentecost illustrates this truth at work. As long as Peter relied on himself he failed the Lord and even denied him. When at last he acknowledged that he had nothing of his own, only the power that was in the name of Jesus, he could heal the man (Acts 3:1–10).

Peter had become "rock," but only after acknowledging that he was spiritually crippled himself, in need of healing and strengthening from Jesus. When the chief among the apostles faced the crippled man, it was the apostolate of cripple to cripple, of the healed one now healing: "Without cost you have received; without cost you are to give" (Matthew 10:8).

Leave Side Altars to the Churches

In the midst of his very beautiful invitation to his disciples to become branches rooted in him, the vine, Jesus says very bluntly, "Without me you can do nothing" (John 15:5). We need constant reminding that we, and our ministerial activity, are to remain centered in Jesus Christ. Our activity is not an end in itself, nor are we defined by it. We cannot and need not save the world, for the simplest of reasons: that has already been done, and by an expert. God's grace works within our call to continue and extend the effects of Christ's saving action in the church and the world.

One implication of our centeredness in Jesus is the priority of our personal relationship with him in prayer in the midst of our individual ministerial activities. Fr. Alan Jones likes to say that there are many ways to avoid taking seriously a deeper spiritual life and union with Christ, and one of the subtlest and most effective is to go into full-time church ministry! He describes this behavior and the healthy approaches to healing it in his work on ministerial spirituality, *Sacrifice and Delight*.[18]

Which brings us to side altars. Many older churches have several side altars—not only the one dedicated to Mary on the left of the main altar, and the one dedicated to Saint Joseph on the right, but others along the side aisles as well. These last are dedicated to patron saints or special devotions, or they may be set aside as Blessed Sacrament chapels. In churches that have been built or renovated more recently, a sparer guideline has dictated one altar only, the altar of sacrifice. I am more prudent than to go into the matter of side altars in a liturgical or architectural sense. My interest in them is only as a lesson for our interior lives as disciples called to share ministerial activity.

Whatever the beauty and merits of side altars architecturally, their equivalents within us are dangerous to our spiritual lives. A "spiritual side altar" can be any project, program, goal, pet idea, vision, ideology, preference, or prejudice to which we find ourselves devoting too much of our time, energy, and attention. And its opponents get more and more of our ill will.

We know that Jesus calls us to make him central to our spiritual lives—the altar of prayer, worship and sacrifice—and to bring directly to him all the yearnings of our hearts and the searchings of our minds. However, if we are not cautious, we can quickly identify much of our value and meaning with what is really only a part of, or a means to, our mission. When we have time for reflection, we can begin to spend it almost entirely at an interior side altar. We may spend that time in exultation and self-congratulation if things are going well, or in anger and resentment if they are not. The point is that we are not centering everything about ourselves on Jesus the Lord, on what he wants, what he is saying to us about his love for us, and how that love for us is to be discerned and responded to in our present situation.

For the faithful disciple, what Jesus values and prefers is what matters most. When we listen with open, humble hearts and minds, he promises to lead us in his way, by his light, to the fullness of his life. Let us listen and follow together, as his disciples.

Pause & Pray

1 Corinthians 1:1–9 Only Jesus Christ, who builds us disciples up into his church, can overcome our human factions.

Notes

1. John Macmurray, quoted by William Barry, S.J., in "The Kingdom of God and Discernment," *America* 157, no. 7 (September 26, 1987), p. 159.

2. Emily Dickinson, "My life closed twice before its close," in *Final Harvest: Emily Dickinson's Poems* (Boston: Little, Brown and Co., 1961), p. 315.

3. T. S. Eliot, "Choruses from 'The Rock,'" *The Complete Poems and Plays, 1909–1950* (New York: Harcourt, Brace and Co., 1952), p. 106.

4. Dorothy Parker, "Re-enter Margot Asquith—A Masterpiece from the French," in *The Portable Dorothy Parker* (New York: Viking Press, 1973), p. 456.

5. Romano Guardini, *The Lord* (Chicago: Henry Regnery Co., 1954), p. 485.

6. "The Ladies Who Lunch," in *Company, a Musical Comedy*, book by George Furth, music and lyrics by Stephen Sondheim (New York: Random House, 1970).

7. Oscar Wilde, *The Importance of Being Earnest* (London: Chiswick Press, 1898), p. 101.

8. J. B. Scaramelli, *Discernimento degli Spiriti* (1753), lists for the discernment of spirits, cited in Kenneth Leech, *Soul Friend: An Invitation to Spiritual Direction* (New York: Harper and Row, 1980), p. 130.

9. Thornton Wilder, *Our Town*, in *Three Plays* (New York: Harper and Bros., 1957), p. 36.

10. Thomas H. Green, S.J., *When The Well Runs Dry* (Notre Dame, Ind.: Ave Maria Press, 1979), pp. 85–86.

11. Enid Bagnold, quoted by T. E. Kalem in "Owl of Wisdom," *Time*, 119, no. 19 (May 10, 1982), p. 116.

12. Gerald May, *Addiction and Grace* (San Francisco: HarperSanFrancisco, 1988), pp. 88–89.

13. Edmond Rostand, *Cyrano de Bergerac*, trans. Brian Hooker (New York: Carlton House, 1923).

14. *Decree on the Apostolate of the Laity*, 1.2, in The *Documents of Vatican II*, gen. ed. Walter M. Abbott, S.J. (New York: Herder and Herder, 1966), p. 491.

15. *Fulfilled in Your Hearing: The Homily in the Sunday Mass Assembly* (Washington, D.C.: United States Catholic Conference, 1982), p. 4.

16. Thomas Merton, introduction to *The Prison Meditations of Father Alfred Delp* (New York: Herder and Herder, 1963), pp. xxvi–xxvii.

17. Ibid.

18. Alan Jones, *Sacrifice and Delight: Spirituality for Ministry* (San Francisco: HarperSanFrancisco, 1992).